Hegemony

Key Concepts in Political Theory series

Charles Jones and Richard Vernon, *Patriotism*
Roger Griffin, *Fascism*
Peter J. Steinberger, *Political Judgment*
Fabian Wendt, *Authority*
Eric Mack, *Libertarianism*
Elizabeth Cohen and Cyril Ghosh, *Citizenship*
Peter Lamb, *Socialism*
Benjamin Moffitt, *Populism*
Mark Stephen Jendrysik, *Utopia*
David D. Roberts, *Totalitarianism*
Peter Lamb, *Property*
Carissa Honeywell, *Anarchism*
Matteo Bonotti and Jonathan Seglow, *Free Speech*
Ian O'Flynn, *Deliberative Democracy*
James Martin, *Hegemony*

Hegemony

James Martin

polity

First published in 2022 by Polity Press

Polity Press
65 Bridge Street
Cambridge CB2 1UR, UK

Polity Press
101 Station Landing
Suite 300
Medford, MA 02155, USA

ISBN-13: 978-1-5095-2160-9
ISBN-13: 978-1-5095-2161-6 (pb)

A catalogue record for this book is available from the British Library.

Library of Congress Control Number: 2021947546

Typeset in 10.5 on 12pt Sabon
by Fakenham Prepress Solutions, Fakenham, Norfolk NR21 8NL
Printed and bound in Great Britain by TJ Books Ltd, Padstow, Cornwall

The publisher has used its best endeavours to ensure that the URLs for external websites referred to in this book are correct and active at the time of going to press. However, the publisher has no responsibility for the websites and can make no guarantee that a site will remain live or that the content is or will remain appropriate.

Every effort has been made to trace all copyright holders, but if any have been overlooked the publisher will be pleased to include any necessary credits in any subsequent reprint or edition.

For further information on Polity, visit our website:
politybooks.com

For my mother

Contents

Acknowledgements   *page* viii

1 What is Hegemony?   1

2 Gramsci: Hegemony and Revolution   13

3 Marxism: Hegemony and the State   36

4 Post-Marxism: Hegemony and Radical Democracy   58

5 Beyond the State: Hegemony in the World   77

6 The End of Hegemony?   96

References   116
Index   127

Acknowledgements

I would like to express my gratitude to a number of people for their help in producing this book: George Owers and Julia Davies at Polity for commissioning it and steering it to completion; my colleague Saul Newman and the publisher's three anonymous reviewers for their comments on an early draft and for suggested revisions; and Susan for some last-minute good sense. Naturally, all responsibility for what follows is mine.

1
What is Hegemony?

Hegemony describes a form of societal leadership whereby those under its influence give assent to domination by a particular group, class, or state. It is used to analyse the informal recognition achieved by certain agents, ideas or arrangements beyond any official status they might claim. Being 'hegemonic' is not merely to occupy power, it is to benefit from widespread acceptance of one's right to rule. In modern political theory, power is usually discussed with reference to particular concepts and principles – for example, authority, legitimacy, rights, and so on – that formally establish and limit it. Hegemony, however, focuses more on actions and processes than principles. It suggests that, fundamentally, relations of power and domination are precarious and endure only by an active ingredient that 'leads' by projecting a unifying purpose and direction.

In recent political theory, hegemony has been something of a 'dissident' concept, employed to expose and challenge, rather than justify, power relations. It is a favoured term of radical critics opposed to dominant social structures and unquestioned beliefs. Focusing on leadership puts the onus on the strategies and techniques by which some agent seeks to transform rivals and opponents into supporters. More than just a description of bare power, then, hegemony invites enquiry into unacknowledged conditions – the social alliances and cultural resources of leadership – that help to institute power relations and make them acceptable, perhaps even desirable. That enquiry is usually undertaken with an understanding that the grip of such leadership can be weakened and domination can be dismantled. Hegemony can also name the objective of those who resist power and seek an alternative, fairer or emancipated, society.

This book introduces some of the notable ways in which hegemony has been used in political theory to analyse power relations and to imagine their transformation. These include reflections on revolutionary strategy, examinations of the capitalist state and its cultural underpinnings, Post-Marxist arguments about 'discourse' and radical democracy, and analyses of world order. In addition to surveying theories, however, it draws attention to important differences in the perceived scope, application, and implications of the concept. Hegemony has been regularly reinvented, refreshed, and reapplied in new contexts. In the process, new formulations emerge, as do questions and conflicts about what type of enquiry it is and to what ends it might be employed.

In tracing the evolution of hegemony as a form of critical enquiry, I underline its role in helping us to ask *questions* about the conditions of power and domination. More than simply providing answers, hegemony challenges us to reflect on how people are implicated in structures of domination and how they might realistically challenge them. So, before sketching the content of the chapters that follow, let me return to the basic analytical issues that underpin hegemony.

Domination as Leadership?

The underlying implication of hegemony is a paradoxical notion: namely, that domination can be experienced as leadership – that is, as a situation to which people give approval despite their apparent subordination. But how can this be so? Usually, domination describes an imbalance of power in which people are subject to a rule that constrains their choices *without* their express agreement. Of course, domination need not always be 'direct' (imposed on us personally) or exercised by one group or individual alone:

states, economic systems, and social arrangements generally entail structures of domination. But what does it mean to say that people 'approve' such constraints?

We might begin by noting that domination is both an objective and a subjective phenomenon. We can speak of it in terms of social conditions that are external to us and independent of our attitudes – the 'facts' of material inequality, the disproportionate presence of white men in positions of institutional authority, empirical evidence of prejudice and violence against specific groups, and so on. But how those conditions are perceived and connected, and therefore whether they are experienced as 'oppressive', is not an automatic consequence of their objective presence. That requires them to be experienced as unacceptable, exploitative, and realistically open to transformation. Yet one consequence of inequalities and hierarchies in power is that those who benefit from them often have the resources to define how everyone's circumstances are interpreted. Or, as Marx and Engels famously put it, 'the ideas of the ruling class are the ruling ideas' (1996: 145). Thus, conditions of systematic constraint or exclusion – which are usually multiple, interwoven, and layered such that they cannot always be viewed as one thing – are frequently justified, defended, and selectively represented in ways that 'naturalize', or at least minimize and isolate, their pernicious effects.

But hegemony is not simply a fictive veneer obscuring naked oppression. Rather than hiding, distracting from, or embellishing an unpleasant reality, it implies something stronger. 'Leadership' suggests a sense of inexorable, collective movement towards a common goal. To lead is to provide unforced direction, to inspire people to endorse certain choices over their own, or even *as* their own. That way, hierarchies and inequalities are perceived not as domination at all, but as acceptable or unavoidable inconveniences. When they are led, people often assume that their ultimate, shared interests are being advanced, that they have a greater stake in what is coming than in how things currently are. Hegemony, I want to suggest, centres on this more encompassing way of understanding the acceptance of domination.

A vital influence here was Antonio Gramsci (1891–1937), the Italian Marxist whose ideas on hegemony from the 1930s offer insights into how social classes seek to exercise what he called 'national-popular' leadership over society. Before Gramsci, hegemony had described, rather narrowly, the 'preeminence' or 'supremacy' of one city state, nation state, or group over others in a political alliance (see Lebow and Kelly 2001; Anderson 2016: 1–11). After its incorporation into debates about revolution, however, Gramsci enriched the concept by making leadership a feature of class domination in general. Classes rule, he argued, not always by forcing others to obey them but by cultivating a broad-based cultural and political consensus – an inclusive sense of belonging – that rationalizes and endorses domination. Gramsci's formulation of hegemony helped others to explain how apparently stable societies were built on certain social alliances and compromises, under the influence of certain cultural values and political ideals. Moreover, hegemony encouraged analysts to identify mechanisms for producing consent (such as the media, culture, and ideology) and to note where, as hegemony waned, forms of conflict and violence were likely to erupt. Many – though not all – later applications of the concept have worked from the ideas developed by Gramsci.

We will look more closely at Gramsci's contribution in chapter 2. But what is important to remember here is that, with him, hegemony describes the paradox of domination – that people accept the leadership of a certain set of figures, ideas, and institutions, despite the domination these support. Unless we appreciate this paradox, then hegemony won't make much sense. Worse, it might be (as it has been) crudely reduced to either the purely objective or the subjective dimensions of domination, in isolation. That is, hegemony might be conceived as either some automatic binding force built in to all power relations without the need to generate leadership, or else as an all-pervasive 'dominant ideology' that is externally imposed to distract people from reality.

But hegemony really only illuminates anything if we regard it as a concept for exploring how, to what extent, and with what resulting tensions the reality of domination and the complexities of experience co-exist. That, I want to suggest, means understanding hegemony as the name for a *practice*, one that operates on different scales, varies in depth and breadth, expands and retracts, and undergoes resistance and reinvention. That is to say, it is another name for politics.

Power, Subjectivity, Ethics

With all this in mind, how are we to explore different approaches to hegemony? Across the twentieth century, debates over hegemony have been moments of innovation in political theory and analysis, as well as occasions for disagreement and controversy. From Gramsci onwards, hegemony has been regularly revised according to new situations and priorities. What is at stake in different approaches is more than just the meaning of a concept, but questions about the shape and mechanisms of social domination and political rule, how to connect objective structures to subjective experiences, and thus how to challenge and reconstitute power anew.

To distinguish approaches to hegemony, we need to review the broad contexts and debates from which they arose. I also suggest we consider how those debates figure three, distinct but overlapping, dimensions of the concept: power, subjectivity, and ethics. These dimensions are present – if unevenly so – in most approaches. There are, of course, other ways to proceed (see, for example, Haugaard and Lentner 2006; Opratko 2012; Worth 2015), but this one encourages a sense of the complexity of the concept while also recognizing its evolution over time. Let us look briefly at each in turn.

Power – a strategic concept

Hegemony, as I've suggested, helps to explain power and domination in terms of the exercise of leadership. Analysing power by reference to the various strategies, contests, and phases in such leadership is one of the concept's most significant contributions to political theory and analysis. It involves a distinctive, 'strategic' concept of power.

In modern political analysis, power has widely been conceived through a theoretical model drawn originally from the natural sciences. Power has been a 'causal concept' (Ball 1975) whereby one independent entity changes the behaviour of another. It is a model introduced in the seventeenth century by Thomas Hobbes, who took it from the (then) new science of mechanics (see Hobbes 1991). To 'hold' power, in his account, is a capacity to make someone act in a way they would not otherwise have chosen. For example, Hobbes understood the Sovereign (or 'Leviathan') as an agent whose overwhelming concentration of power causes others to obey. Since then, that model of power – understood as a 'zero-sum' possession with causal properties – has been paradigmatic for social and political analysts, even when they disagree about who possesses it or how it operates (Clegg 1989).

But the causal model cannot really explain human behaviour. Undoubtedly, some individuals, groups or organizations concentrate resources, which gives them a greater ability to shape others' actions. But humans are not mindless 'objects in motion' whose interactions are externally determined. They are agents who create and share meaning, and their actions are conditioned by their self-understanding, and so by the conceptual and linguistic terms and rule-based frameworks they employ. Behaviour is mediated by symbolic constructions that dispose towards – not 'determine' – some choices over others. The causal model of power is a metaphor that does not helpfully grasp the varied and complex ways in which symbols can 'shape', 'influence', 'urge', 'threaten', 'encourage' or 'provoke' behaviour (Ball 1975). These terms describe *reasons*, not causes. Because behaviour is subjectively mediated, it is usually impossible to isolate a single, independent 'cause' that acts externally upon individuals.

Hegemony, by contrast, invokes a model of power that we can call 'strategic'. That model, as described by Clegg (1989: 29–34), rejects the notion of power as a causal force concentrated in one place, as Hobbes argued. Instead, it treats power as an evolving and unstable field of forces. The strategic model derives from the work of the sixteenth-century political thinker Niccolò Machiavelli. For him, power was never fully captured or possessed by any one agent (see Machiavelli 1988). Rather, politics was characterized by shifting strengths and concentrations of resource, in which changing abilities and fluctuating opportunities perpetually alter wider relations, and make the exercise of 'dominion' provisional. Machiavelli therefore treated political analysis as the interpretation of changing strategies of rule, not the advocacy of a single structure to order society (see Clegg 1989: 34–6).

Hegemony, I want to suggest, aligns with Machiavelli's strategic model of power more than it does with Hobbes' causal account. That makes it problematic for those who conceive power and domination as emanating from an objective and unitary structure. To exercise hegemony is to be in a temporary relation of supremacy over others, not in absolute possession of power. That is not to deny the existence of structures of domination and concentrations of power. But such forces are only ever partially effective and require active support to sustain them. Hegemony directs attention, then, to the strategies, practices, and networks of influence that achieve this. But, in so doing, it transforms the idea of power as absolute mastery into something less precise: a terrain or field of relations whose various parts do not automatically cohere but are, momentarily, held in balance.

The strategic view of power, we might say, is more like a battlefield than a castle – its parameters shift as allies are made and lost, as key strongholds are taken or relinquished, and as patterns of influence expand and retract. We need to ask what is the *scope* of hegemony? Who are its agents? What are its techniques? To what degree do concentrations of power – such as the state, capitalism, or patriarchy – rely on consensual leadership, and when do they employ coercion? Is there only ever one system of hegemony or can there be many? These are matters of interpretation that vary according to the focus and application of the concept.

Subjectivity – capturing experience

'Subjectivity' refers to how we experience the world – the ways in which our conscious reactions and attitudes are defined and organized through knowledge, moral values, sentiments, or desires. Hegemony's focus on leadership places emphasis on how these aspects of subjectivity are recruited to support, or oppose, forms of rule. It demands that we think about humans as relatively independent subjects, not as objects that act according to prescribed behaviours derived from their social position.

Hegemony is often associated with categories such as 'ideology', 'culture', or 'discourse' since those describe the broad domains where meanings circulate and are contested. Ideology, in particular, carries both the 'neutral' meaning of systems of belief that provide more or less coherent views of the world, *and* the more 'critical' sense of false or partial ideas that mislead people about reality, thereby servicing particular interests. Hegemony combines both senses in so far as some privileged group is often identified as the benefactor of hegemony, though this does not require that all ideas and beliefs are reducible to its interests. One key claim in theories of hegemony is that it succeeds to the extent that people come to experience their world, unquestioningly, through the prism of a dominant group's preferred categories and concepts (or ideology), which are then accepted as 'natural' or 'universal'.

Our focus, then, might sometimes be the group that benefits from this leadership. But it also might be on the ways other groups and practices come to be led. Some of the most inventive uses of hegemony have been by scholars of cultural studies such as Raymond Williams or Stuart Hall, for whom popular experiences of 'everyday life', 'culture', or 'common sense' (as Gramsci called it) were the locus for ongoing negotiations with dominant social forces. Hegemony, in their analyses, encourages us to ask how seemingly disparate forms of cultural activity – such as writing, cinema, or music – are implicated in contests to determine what it is that society holds in common.

The question of subjectivity is, however, controversial. It requires that we account for how symbols function, how they become activated and deployed (when, and by what mechanisms?), and how they contribute to the persistence (or not) of particular structures of domination. How does ideology or culture relate to social interests (which are assumed to be more or less fixed)? Indeed, what are the limits of this feature of leadership? Hegemony implies that domination is not easily demarcated around one discrete agent but, rather, subtly entangled in the subjectivity of ordinary people via language or forms of cultural attachment. That makes it difficult to identify a single 'owner' of ideas or benefactor of power. The complex relation of subjects to forms of violence and coercion is also pertinent here since hegemony rejects exclusive attention to coercion in favour of consent. Yet violence is frequently a feature of struggles over hegemonic leadership – especially when some groups resist it – and sometimes a sign of its internal fracturing. Social crises, when alliances splinter and once-shared values fall into open dispute, may express the subjective symptoms of hegemonic decline.

Ethics – uniting leaders and led

Finally, hegemony implies an ethical relationship that governs the interactions between leading groups and their key allies and supporters.

Most uses of hegemony are focused on analysing strategic features of domination. They tend not to be overtly 'normative' or deal with moral questions. Indeed, theorists of hegemony are usually moral 'realists' in that respect, treating normative issues as inseparable from practical problems posed by empirical reality. Nonetheless, leadership usually involves expressing common ideals as well as internally organizing and regulating how different groups and interests relate through them. Priority might be given to certain types of association – class solidarity, national identity, democratic respect – that connect hegemony's politics to an ethic that assists the integration of its various parts.

Hegemonic strategies raise questions about how leaders enact their responsibility to the forces that sustain them. What kinds of elites rule, and from where do they originate? How is popular experience incorporated into the ways they lead? What relationship do supporting groups have with each other? The ethical dimension of hegemony is particularly relevant to those who wish to substitute domination with an alternative, 'democratic' or 'liberated', order. But it is not always examined closely, possibly because normative commitments are frequently presupposed as given. The question of what ethical terms organize hegemony is, however, a lively issue when old solidarities and modes of participation can no longer be taken for granted. Of note here is the question of the extent to which strategies of hegemony are compatible with pluralistic, democratic ideals.

Hegemony is a powerful concept because it condenses into one term a variety of complex phenomena. It is probably wise, then, to think of it not simply as a concept in the abstract but as the name for a general framework for examining the interaction of these different dimensions. Doing so can help us to draw attention to the different accents and emphases that have characterized its use.

Chapter Outline

The following chapters explore five themes that, in broadly chronological order, have defined new formulations and applications of, or debates about, hegemony. Each chapter deals with a distinct framing of arguments and issues in the evolution of the concept. But the themes are also topics that extend across time and serve as the preferred frame for readers to think about hegemony. So the chapters can be read sequentially or, if preferred, according to the theme that interests you most.

Chapter 2 begins with the seminal work of Antonio Gramsci, who supplied the basic coordinates for many contemporary reflections on hegemony. For him, it was a concept that helped to elaborate a distinctive strategy for revolution in developed capitalist states. That strategy was conceived as a process of consensual state-building rather than a Bolshevik-style, violent seizure of power. It meant gradually extending the cultural and political bases of support for an emergent ruling class. In Gramsci's work, hegemony expands into a whole framework of analysis for understanding the origins, techniques, and limits of class domination.

In chapter 3, our focus is on Marxist debates over how to apply hegemony to the analysis of the postwar capitalist state. Unlike Gramsci, who wrote during a period of political instability, thinkers in the 1960s and 1970s utilized hegemony to understand the evolution of relatively stable 'welfare' states. Hegemony helped to focus on the political integrity of national capitalisms, but also on their changing cultural foundations and sites of ideological tension. Marxist theories of the capitalist state and the emergent discipline of cultural studies each made important contributions to the development of the concept in this period. Their analyses were crucial for understanding efforts to rebuild social bases of consent, such as the phenomenon of 'Thatcherism' in the 1980s and, more recently, forms of right-wing 'populism'.

'Post-Marxist' approaches to hegemony are the theme of chapter 4. The project of 'radical democracy' initiated by Ernesto Laclau and Chantal Mouffe involved a major theoretical reconstruction of hegemony as a framework of analysis and a strategy for emancipation. The obsolescence, as they saw it, of Marxist appeals to economic 'determination' and to the political primacy of class demanded new ways to theorize radical politics. Coming near the end of the Cold War and just in advance of the collapse of South African Apartheid, Post-Marxism and radical democracy looked forward, presciently, to a non-revolutionary, pluralist politics of social movements. In Post-Marxist approaches, hegemony became more theoretical but also more mobile, exploring diverse forms of power and domination, numerous different 'discourses', and political contests.

In chapter 5, we consider the application of hegemony to the study of international politics. Hegemony has a different lineage here. In theories of International Relations, it has been widely used by so-called 'realist' scholars to explain the leading role of a dominant world power in a system of states. That approach was challenged by radical critics – notably, Robert W. Cox – who drew on Gramsci's insights to reconnect international politics to class struggles within world capitalism. Neo-Gramscian scholars of International Political Economy have subsequently explored the historical, political, and ideological dimensions of international hegemony. They have contributed to the analysis and critique of 'globalization', understood as an expansion of 'neo-liberal' capitalism.

Finally, chapter 6 turns its attention to critiques of hegemony by recent political theorists. Despite regular reinvention, hegemony is tied to a view of political power as something to be identified, challenged, and remade. For a number of critics, however, the language of hegemony – particularly its preoccupation with strategies that unify people and join them in a common project – remains a project of mastery. Indeed, it is argued – on the basis of radically different 'ontological' grounds – that hegemony cannot appreciate the dynamic nature of power and the 'spontaneous', 'autonomous,' and creative forms of resistance to it. A genuinely radical politics, it is proposed by various 'new materialists' and anarchists, demands not the reinvention but the end of hegemony.

2
Gramsci: Hegemony and Revolution

Hegemony is widely associated with the genius of Antonio Gramsci, the Italian revolutionary incarcerated by Mussolini's Fascist regime in the 1920s and 1930s. Of course, he did not invent the term but, more accurately, *reinvented* it in the notes and essays he wrote during a lengthy spell in prison that, eventually, killed him. In those writings, Gramsci employed 'hegemony' to reimagine revolution as a process of building popular consent to a new form of state.

But why would Gramsci pursue a theory about consent while under conditions of physical coercion? Surely, his incarceration is evidence that force is the ultimate tool of social control? Gramsci's point was that even authoritarian regimes such as Fascism, which ruled Italy for twenty years, needed willing support across *some* sectors of society. Modern states, he argued, increasingly aspire to 'intellectual and moral leadership' of their populations, however much physical force is also required. The capacity to lead by consent was what he called 'hegemony' (*egemonia*) and, in class-divided societies like Italy's, it was usually combined with degrees of coercion. As we shall see, Gramsci was a communist so, for him, hegemony helped in exploring the conditions for leading a revolution to overthrow capitalism. It put into perspective how a whole socio-political order could be established, sustained, or transformed. His prison writings offer a comprehensive account of how domination is entwined with elements of political and cultural leadership. For that reason, Gramsci's insights are a major benchmark in the fortunes of hegemony.

Gramsci's Fusion

Gramsci drew upon two prominent intellectual traditions in developing his ideas. As a Marxist, he shared in a tradition of revolutionary thought that conceived social classes as the primary agents of historical change. In particular, he was influenced by the Bolsheviks, led by Vladimir Ilyich 'Lenin', who in October 1917 successfully overthrew the Tsarist regime in Russia. The Russian Revolution was of enormous significance for Gramsci and his generation. It was demonstrable proof that an entire political order could be replaced through organized mass action. Lenin provided a model of revolution that centred on the 'vanguard' party – a disciplined, centralized organization of professional revolutionaries that led, on behalf of the working class, the effort to overthrow the state and instil a new order (Lenin 1992). In debating the conditions for revolution, particularly in countries with partial capitalist development, Lenin and other Russian Marxists had used 'hegemony' to describe the leading role of the working class over its allies in preparing for the seizure of power (see Anderson 1976–7; Lester 2000: 29–51).

Gramsci also inherited ideas rooted in a distinctively Italian political tradition that stretched back to Niccolò Machiavelli (see Fontana 1993). In that tradition, politics was conceived as an ongoing process of building and maintaining a state, securing and extending its rule over potential rivals. Italian thinkers frequently employed the dichotomy of force and consent to understand authority (Femia 1998). Rather than imagine a 'social contract' as the founding principle of legitimate rule – which established domination once and for all – they understood authority to be intrinsically unstable. Politics was a constant practice of maintaining power by pragmatically balancing brute force and willing consent. It did not matter, strictly speaking, what motivated consent:

fear, love, or self-interest were all much the same. When nineteenth-century Italian thinkers later employed hegemony to imagine the nation state, they did so in this sense of stealthily expanding consent, rather than force alone, over an otherwise fractious and culturally divided society (Jacobitti 1981).

So 'hegemony' was already a term in use before Gramsci appropriated it. It underscored the strategic priorities in founding and maintaining political order where authority could not be taken for granted – either through the primacy of one class in leading a coalition (Russia) or cumulatively extending a national base of support (Italy). Gramsci fused these traditions in a unique way. Revolution in developed capitalism, he argued, should not be aimed, narrowly, at the violent seizure of power (as Russian revolutionaries argued). Rather, it entailed preparing a new order by displacing an existing hegemony and cultivating a new one. But that did not mean espousing some benign, but empty, ideal of 'national unity'. At the root of any hegemony was an effort to generate a collective subject from the material conditions and experiences of a distinct social class.

In his prison writings, Gramsci combined these ideas to assemble a distinctive vocabulary for exploring politics as a struggle for hegemony: 'integral state', 'war of position' and 'war of manoeuvre', 'historic bloc', 'passive revolution', and so on. These terms form an essential part of his legacy and are vital to its later applications. But, as I shall note, his framework also contains unresolved tensions and challenges for those who want to take them further.

Revolution and the Italian State

What prompted Gramsci to develop the concept of hegemony? Of all the places to begin thinking about hegemony, Italy in the early twentieth century may seem the most unlikely. The 'liberal' state – formally unified by 1871 – was notoriously weak and unpopular. The Catholic Church refused to recognize its authority, political elites were aloof from the wider public, and governments were inclined to impose order on society by force. Italy's new citizens were, in turn, resentful of its power over them and frequently resisted it. This was a country of regions, diverse local cultures, multiple dialects, and profound material inequality. That was especially so in its underdeveloped, rural South where the new state was often experienced as a colonial force (Clark 1984). Italy had been legally unified, yet – *contra* the national communion envisioned by advocates of unification, such as Giuseppe Mazzini – in reality the liberal order remained precarious.

It was because the liberal state was built *without* widespread popular consent – no 'civil religion' or national sentiment unified it – that Gramsci eventually elaborated his own approach to hegemony (Bellamy and Schecter 1993). His aspiration, like that of so many radical intellectuals angry at a glaringly incomplete unification, was to replace this liberal order on 'the periphery of modernity' (Urbinati 1998) with one that properly incorporated its popular classes – mostly peasants who worked on the land, as well as a small industrial working class concentrated in the North. Like others, too, he saw this as a process of generating a modern ruling class responsive to the lives and needs of ordinary people (see Bellamy 1987).

Gramsci had been born to a family of Albanian descent on the island of Sardinia, in Italy's South. He witnessed, first-hand, the liberal state's social and administrative inadequacies – its chronic poverty, the contempt of its rulers for people's lives, and the corrupt, inefficient ways the regime functioned (Davidson 1977). After moving, in 1911, to the northern city of Turin, he became a socialist, committed to overthrowing capitalism and modernizing the state. Gramsci was soon a radical journalist and commentator. A speaker of Sardinian and a student of linguistics at university, he was – unlike most socialists – uniquely attuned to the country's fragmented national culture (see Ives 2004). For him, revolution was the only way properly to integrate the mass of the population into a political order with a shared ethos, like more developed states such as Britain and France. Socialism therefore meant educating the working classes into a morally disciplined community to lead the nation as a whole. He therefore rejected the dominant Marxist tradition, whose crude 'scientific' doctrine assumed the so-called 'iron laws' of history would bring about capitalism's inevitable collapse. The young Gramsci was influenced, instead, by 'idealists' who emphasized the importance of cultural education, moral rigour, and the power of the will in shaping history (see Bellamy 1990).

The First World War unleashed a profound, levelling violence that shattered Europe's systems of class hierarchies and closed, elite politics. As imperial powers and constitutional monarchies across Europe tottered under the pressure of popular resentments, Gramsci judged the Italian liberal order to be effectively obsolete (Vacca 2020). In Italy in 1919–20, sustained strikes and factory occupations brought industry to a standstill. Similar uprisings took place in Germany and Hungary. Gramsci saw a chance for workers to begin generating *their own* form of state within the organization of industrial production (Gramsci 1977). Inspired by the Russian Revolution and its 'soviet' system of workers' councils, he argued that Italy's factories might prefigure a new form of democratic authority based on workers' self-management (see Clark 1979; Schecter 1991). A shared mentality as 'producers', he claimed, could replace the abstract idea of the 'citizen', and an integrated system of planned industrial production would substitute for the aimless chatter of parliament.

When the industrial unrest eventually came to an end, intense anti-socialist and anti-democratic reaction set in, as it did elsewhere in Europe (Morgan 2003: 29–63). Gangs of returning servicemen and various unsavoury thugs undertook violent reprisals against workers across Italy, burning down socialist properties and terrorizing rural towns, often with the tacit support of local authorities (Lyttelton 1973). Benito Mussolini – a former revolutionary socialist turned radical nationalist – soon manoeuvred his Fascist Party into government by stoking violent disorder and winning support from middle classes fearful of socialist revolution. Still hopeful that events could be turned to revolution, Gramsci and other communist sympathizers abandoned the Italian Socialist Party to found the Communist Party of Italy (PCI) in 1921. Organized in the mould of the Bolsheviks under Lenin – with strict discipline and ideological rigidity – it sought a clear break with 'reformist' socialism and dismissed the Fascists as reactionary stooges of the old order.

But the arrival of Fascism in Italy was a disaster not only for the liberals who ushered Mussolini into power, hoping to manipulate him for their own ends, but for anyone looking to reorganize the Italian state democratically. As Prime Minister, Mussolini soon tightened his grip, discarding parliamentary democracy and arresting dissenters. All civil and political opposition was eventually crushed and *Il Duce* projected himself as the incarnation of the popular will. The Fascists then began to build an authoritarian order around a mass-based cult of the nation.

Gramsci realized that the left's divisions, its isolation from the wider public, and its underestimation of the Fascists had been mistakes. He took on the role of the general secretary of the PCI in 1923 and began to rethink revolutionary strategy. Rather than rely on a catastrophic collapse of capitalism, he argued, communists needed to organize across society, forge alliances with sympathetic intellectuals, disaffected groups and classes, and lead an anti-Fascist 'united front' of workers and peasants (see Gramsci 1978: 372–5). He began to use the term 'hegemony' to describe this strategy, taking it directly from Russian debates. Yet, the Bolshevik model of revolution, he implied, was inadequate for more developed states, even for peripheral capitalist states like Italy's with a large peasant population under the sway of an agrarian bloc of landowners, and supported by southern 'intellectuals' (1978: 441–62). Instead of organizing to seize power, communists needed to sink roots into society and prepare for the long term.

Unfortunately for Gramsci, that strategy had no chance of taking off. In 1926, he was arrested by the authorities and sentenced to over twenty years in prison for opposing the regime. For many political prisoners, that would have been the end of the road. But Gramsci was granted access to writing materials and, later, to a prison library. Between 1929 and 1935, he filled nearly 3,000 pages in twenty-nine, hand-written notebooks with his thoughts and reflections (see Gramsci 1971 and 1995). It is there that we find a more sophisticated elaboration of the idea of hegemony.

Hegemony and the Prison Notebooks

What are Gramsci's *Prison Notebooks* about? They comprise a substantial variety of essays and notes, often partially revised over the years, where he sketched his evolving thoughts on themes such as intellectuals, Italian history, language and culture, the revolutionary party, philosophy, and economics. These may appear disparate topics, but they converge around strategic issues and concerns which had preoccupied him prior to his arrest. For most scholars, hegemony forms their unifying thread (Femia 1981; Schwarzmantel 2015).

In his *Notebooks*, Gramsci distinguished political strategies aimed at building support across society from those that did not, or did so only partially. One of his primary targets in this was 'scientific' Marxism, which reasoned from abstract principles and generic historic 'laws' with little regard to concrete particularities. Such views – which he rubbished as 'primitive infantilism' – remained influential among Marxists in the international communist movement and, in his view, hampered proper understanding of strategic conditions in different states. Gramsci formulated his account of hegemony as a comprehensive critique of Marxist 'economism' (or determinism and reductionism), insisting on the need to be attentive to real historical circumstances in preparing revolution.

Gramsci's thinking about hegemony in the *Notebooks* involved a number of overlapping themes: a general concept of politics understood as a process of cultural state-building by expanding consensual support, applicable generally to any social class trying to seal its domination; the importance of ideology and subjective experience as the medium through which hegemony is generated and contested; and the idea of the revolutionary party as a 'Modern Prince' (in reference to Machiavelli's image of a wily political leader), and the architect of a new 'national-popular collective will'. Together, these themes cover much of the impressive breadth of Gramsci's thought. Let us look at each in turn.

Building consent: state and civil society

In the *Notebooks*, 'hegemony' describes a dynamic, historical process of building a state by extending leadership across civil society. We have noted that, even before incarceration, Gramsci had begun to focus on the social bases of support that distinguished revolution in the developed West from the Russian experience. In his *Notebooks*, he expanded this insight into a *general* principle of a modern politics since the late nineteenth century. In 'the case of most advanced states', he claims, '"civil society" has become a very complex structure ... resistant to catastrophic "incursions" of the immediate economic element (crises, depressions, etc.). The superstructures of civil society are like the trench-systems of modern warfare' (1971: 235).

In this military analogy, the so-called 'trenches' of civil society include newspapers, churches, clubs and other civil associations – a whole variety of 'private' organizations that are formally independent of public authority but, nonetheless, function as an unofficial 'line of defence' to preserve state power from social disruption. It is the presence of a developed civil society, for Gramsci, that marked the crucial distinction between advanced capitalist countries and those like Russia. Using similar language, he reasserted this point in terms of revolution in the 'East' (that is, Russia) and the 'West' (Western Europe):

> In the East the state was everything, civil society was primordial and gelatinous; in the West, there was a proper relation between State and civil society, and when the State trembled a sturdy structure of civil society was at once revealed. The State was only an outer ditch, behind which there stood a powerful system of fortresses and earthworks. (1971: 238)

The modern state in advanced capitalist democracies (not necessarily geographically located in the West), he suggests, is partially shielded from direct public hostility by 'complexes of associations in civil society' that reinforce its rule. These reduce the need to deploy direct force to ensure public obedience. That is not to say that force is *never* required. But as civil society becomes more supportive, recourse to violence is rendered 'partial' – unnecessary except in isolated instances (1971: 243). When crises come, they are, consequently, less damaging to state authority. The 'sturdy structure of civil society', he asserts, functions to protect the formal apparatuses of executive power.

Gramsci's formulations on the relation between state and civil society mark an important break with the received Marxist tradition, which in the *Communist Manifesto* had conceived the state (understood as a single, unified agency) as the coordinating centre and coercive apparatus of class power (see Marx and Engels 1996). By insisting on the significance of civil society, he formulated a more complex notion. More than just a source of violence, a state comprises 'the entire complex of practical and theoretical activities with which the ruling class not only justifies and maintains its dominance, but manages to win the active consent of those over whom it rules' (1971: 244). A modern state seeks not just fearful obedience but, moreover, popular consent. By exhorting norms and values – such as the virtues of legality, moral integrity, national identity – it builds support with a common ethos 'to create and maintain a certain type of civilisation and of citizen' (1971: 246). Thus, the state is an 'educator', not just a brute defender of power. If its authority is ultimately underpinned by law and violence, nonetheless it normally undertakes a positive, 'civilising activity' (1971: 247).

How does the modern state generate this consent? As an educator, promoting an inclusive, national way of life, it usually undertakes public schooling directly to inculcate its citizens into common values. But, Gramsci noted, such values were also indirectly promoted *outside* of formal public instruction by 'private initiatives and activities', such as churches, newspapers, and professional organizations. These, he noted, 'form the apparatus of the political and cultural hegemony of the ruling classes' (1971: 258). They supply an informal but extensive network of supportive organizations that nourish a system of values. This was precisely what Italian thinkers had felt was lacking after unification – or what philosophers influenced by Hegel called an 'ethical state' to extend popular consent and cultivate citizenship.

Gramsci's remarks on state and civil society incorporate this distinctively Italian preoccupation with state-building into his reflections on revolution. Revolution is consequently re-conceived, not as an assault on the bastions of class power, as it was for Lenin, but as a *process* of expanding cultural influence, rendering secondary the element of violence. In the *Notebooks*, we see that idea repeatedly formulated as a general political principle.

In his notes on Italian history, for example, Gramsci remarks that: 'the supremacy of a social group manifests itself in two ways, as "domination" and as "intellectual and moral leadership". A social group dominates antagonistic groups, which it tends to "liquidate", or to subjugate perhaps even by armed force; it leads kindred and allied groups.' Here is the classic distinction, noted earlier, between force and consent. But Gramsci goes on to assert: 'A social group can, and indeed must, already exercise "leadership" before winning governmental power (this indeed is one of the principal conditions for the winning of such power); it subsequently becomes dominant when it exercises power, but even if it holds it firmly in its grasp, it must continue to "lead" as well' (1971: 57–8).

Achieving hegemony over civil society, Gramsci suggests, is not secondary to taking power but, rather, a *precondition* for it. That remark is made in a series of notes on bourgeois revolutions in the nineteenth century. In the French Revolution, he observes, the radical 'Jacobins' built their own base of support to defeat the *Ancien Régime*: 'not only did they organise a bourgeois government, i.e. make the bourgeoisie the dominant class – they did more. They created the bourgeois State, made the bourgeoisie into the leading, hegemonic class of the nation, in other words gave the new State a permanent basis and created the compact modern French nation' (1971: 79). Gramsci's implication is that, like the bourgeoisie, communists must think of revolution this way – not merely 'occupying' the state but leading, in advance (but also thereafter), across civil society.

Gramsci's remarks on state and civil society are a significant innovation in the Marxist idea of politics. The state, for him, is not a naked 'dictatorship' of the bourgeoisie, amassing all its material and financial resources to impose order. Rather, it denotes a larger space of contest inside which political groups and classes contend for 'supremacy' by sustaining a coalition of different interests and developing a unifying culture. Gramsci even defines the state in what he calls 'its integral meaning' as 'dictatorship + hegemony' (1971: 239), or force plus consent: 'in other words, one might say that State = political society + civil society, in other words hegemony protected by the armour of coercion' (1971: 263). In this 'general' or 'integral' sense, which now blurs the boundaries of the state, civil society is regarded as 'the State itself', in so far as it effectively binds society to its authority (1971: 261).

The primary focus of revolutionary attention, then, cannot be confrontation with the state's coercive apparatus but, rather, engagement with the more ambiguous, loosely organized terrain of allied classes, groups and civil associations over which hegemony is exercised. In Gramsci's analysis, it is vital to gauge the complex 'relations of forces' that uphold bourgeois power (1971: 180–5). That approach signals a switch from what he calls – sticking with his military metaphors – the 'war of manoeuvre' (or 'war of movement') to the 'war of position'. The war of manoeuvre describes a frontal attack on the enemy – but a war of position involves gradually taking key positions around the enemy. Gramsci notes that, in politics, winning those positions is 'decisive definitively' (1971: 239). That is to say, revolutionary strategy should transform the strongholds of hegemony into its own support. Despite the military language – which was common among revolutionaries – Gramsci was clear that 'politics ... must have priority' for 'only politics creates the possibility for manoeuvre and movement' (1971: 232). Marxists, he insisted, need to speak a nuanced language of political struggle, and not only that of military conquest.

Gramsci's insistence on acquiring a rigorous, political understanding of the revolutionary process was more than a reiteration of the priority to form alliances, as implied in Russian debates about hegemony. He recast the very idea of class power. Gramsci rejected Marxism's status as a purely 'objective' analysis of the overall economic determination of society (1971: 407, 412). Although economic classes and social structures are the underlying context of all domination, he refuses any mono-causal account that asserts that an economic 'base' directly determines the cultural and political 'superstructure'. The components of the superstructure (civil society, the state, ideology) are not a secondary reflection of class interests, nor did they follow, uniformly, imperatives imposed by economic structures. Rather than talk of 'base' and 'superstructure', Gramsci offered the term 'historic bloc' to describe how economic structures and political initiatives (i.e. degrees of hegemonic influence) are dialectically interwoven in concrete conditions (1971: 137, 168). Class domination is never an automatic extension of economic power, but a precarious, political and cultural achievement, as it gradually expands its influence beyond the sphere of production relations to generate an ethical state of its own.

Intellectuals, ideology, and common sense

How is consensual leadership extended over civil society? Gramsci placed particular emphasis on the importance of human *consciousness* in building hegemony. Here, again, he was critical of crude Marxist models of class and ideology. If 'subaltern' (or subordinate) social classes could be won over by a dominant class, then ideas and beliefs were not a strict 'reflection' of pre-given interests. Reviving his long-standing appreciation of language, Gramsci argued that ideology was neither a mirror of class nor, on the other hand, merely a 'false consciousness' obscuring reality (see Ives 2004: 72–101). On the contrary, 'popular beliefs', folklore, shared mentalities, and perceptions all have a psychological 'validity' in so far as they help to practically 'organise' people and enable them to 'acquire consciousness of their position, struggle, etc.' (Gramsci 1971: 377). Such outlooks – often embedded in commonplace phrases and words – have multiple sources and mediate people's reception of social and political power. Understanding any existing or potential hegemony therefore meant grasping this subjective terrain as something to be organized and led.

At the centre of Gramsci's concerns here was the category of intellectuals, which forms a major theme throughout the *Notebooks*. Like many Italian thinkers, Gramsci perceived politics in terms of the activities of elites. Notoriously, that was the preoccupation of political scientists Vilfredo Pareto and Gaetano Mosca, who regarded small groups of elites as the inevitable agents of political power (see Femia 1998). But Italian philosophers generally assumed that types of elite – such as artists or national figures – bore particular responsibility for promoting and disseminating a shared worldview. Leadership in national politics and culture was frequently viewed as the exercise of influence by a superior elite over the disorganized 'masses'.

For Gramsci, likewise, the work of state-building is undertaken by intellectuals who provide the conceptual frameworks that give to a class its sense of 'homogeneity' and self-awareness as a distinct social force (1971: 5): 'Critical self-consciousness means, historically and politically, the creation of an élite of intellectuals' (1971: 334). Intellectuals are not, he points out, necessarily academics or super-brained geniuses (which he refers to as 'traditional' intellectuals) but 'organisers and leaders' – anyone with a specialized role in communicating and justifying knowledge to others and shaping their moral conduct. 'All men are intellectuals', he notes, in so far as they think and share in a conception of the world, 'but not all men have in society the function of intellectuals' (1971: 9) – they need not be academics or philosophers, but they do need to be communicators able to connect local, practical activities to an encompassing vision of social and political life. Intellectuals are 'the dominant group's "deputies" exercising the subaltern functions of social hegemony and political government' (1971: 12).

Different historical conjunctures and different modes of economic organization generate their own categories of 'organic intellectual' – managers, engineers, instructors, and so on (see 1971: 14–15). They translate concrete tasks associated with a social class (such as banking and finance, trade, or innovations in production) into a more accessible language that ensures the '"spontaneous" consent given by the great masses of the population to the general direction imposed on social life by the dominant fundamental group' (1971: 12). Alongside them will be 'traditional intellectuals' who represent earlier modes of organizing knowledge (such as clerics or professors). Thus, the content of the category changes over time as new intellectuals emerge to rationalize class economic functions as integral to the political order (1971: 334).

Intellectuals, Gramsci maintains, impose conceptual order and coherence on the less well-organized thinking of ordinary people. To lead, a class must usually elaborate its own 'philosophy' in popular form rather than keep it a purely specialized knowledge for a restricted few. That is to say, a hegemonic culture is one that resonates with the problems experienced by subordinate classes who, left unorganized, will hold to 'contradictory' and undeveloped beliefs, superstitions, or customs (1971: 326, 333). Ordinary 'conceptions of the world', Gramsci observed, were typically fragmentary and incoherent, 'fossilised and anachronistic' (1971: 325), the legacy of relations of 'submission and intellectual subordination' (1971: 327). Man is 'a précis of the past', a layered 'synthesis' of current and past social relations (1971: 353) without internal order. People usually live their practical existences through unexamined 'common sense' phrases and opinions that guide their immediate attitudes but obscure their relation to structures of power, often making them 'fatalistic'. There is, Gramsci argues, a basis of 'good sense' – or practical rationality – in such beliefs, but that is often lost, and what remains are stale propositions that lack critical reflection (1971: 348).

The task of the intellectual, then, is to bring order to common sense by connecting it to a more developed, internally consistent philosophy. That is not to say common sense is simply abandoned. For Gramsci, ordinary people are not likely to renounce their usual modes of thinking, which endure as instinctual attachments and passionate beliefs: 'in the masses *as such*, philosophy can only be experienced as a faith' (1971: 339). The functional division between 'intellectuals' and 'masses' would therefore always remain. But any hegemonic ideology will be built both on a coherent philosophy *and* on already existing forms of common sense, so as to enter into the 'life' of ordinary people. In that respect, the contest for hegemony, as Gramsci envisaged it, involves 'educating' popular attitudes and prejudices, imposing coherence on them, and re-working existing beliefs to fit with new forms of 'intellectual and moral order' (1971: 325).

Revolutionary ethics: the 'Modern Prince'

How, according to Gramsci, is a new hegemony to be organized? In customary Leninist fashion, it is the revolutionary party that is allocated that task. After Machiavelli's text *The Prince*, Gramsci imagined the Communist Party as a 'Modern Prince' – the collective founder of a state gathering 'subaltern' classes into a vision of a new proletarian civilization. The Party, in Gramsci's view, must become a 'Jacobin force', awakening a 'national-popular collective will' (1971: 131) connecting organic intellectuals by disseminating a new 'myth' or 'world-view' (1971: 132). In that respect, hegemony implies an *ethical* outlook, albeit one wrapped in the language of political objectives and necessities. Gramsci didn't write as a moral thinker, but hegemony is nonetheless 'ethical-political' since any such strategy is inseparable from some model of civil association.

For Gramsci, the Party's objective must be the transformation of society in a way that overcomes rigid distinctions between leaders and led, or 'elites' and 'masses'. Otherwise, social transformation threatens to become a 'passive revolution' – replacing the ruling class without actively mobilizing the wider population (1971: 106–14). That had been the underlying problem of Italian unification, and it was possible, too, in the Soviet Union under Stalin (see Vacca 2020: ch. 2). Gramsci's language in the *Notebooks* oscillates between one of military strategy and one of cultural and educational development. The Modern Prince is a peculiar hybrid: leading a centrally directed coalition of forces, calculating its tactics in light of the prevailing 'relations of force' – but also nurturing a mass following, preparing a new type of collective subject based on non-hierarchical principles.

How are these different aims to be reconciled? Gramsci was critical of a permanent separation of leaders and led. But he was convinced that some distinction remained necessary: 'there really do exist rulers and ruled, leaders and led. The entire science and art of politics are based on this primordial, and (given certain conditions) irreducible fact' (1971: 144). So, his model of the Party insisted on disciplined, hierarchical organization, while also permitting the circulation of ideas and personnel. A mass of intellectuals and ordinary members are required if the Party is to embed itself across civil society. They are the recipients of its ideas and the medium to transmit a new common sense. Without them, Party doctrine would be a series of unchallenged philosophical pronouncements delivered from on-high to a passive, 'unquestioning' membership (1971: 145). So the Party must organize in the industrial factories and the communities of the proletariat and peasantry.

But the Party must also find organic intellectuals who can grasp sophisticated, technical theories and principles (such as Marxism) and transmit them to ordinary members and allies. Gramsci devoted a whole notebook to the phenomenon he labelled 'Americanism and Fordism' – the 'scientifically' managed system of mass production advocated by Frederick W. Taylor and utilized by Henry Ford in the US (see 1971: 279–318). That system could provide the economic foundation to a future hegemony, disciplining workers and developing new leaders from among technical specialists and managers: 'Intellectual and moral reform has to be linked with a programme of economic reform' (1971: 133).

But the workers needed to be led, not left to emerge 'spontaneously'. The Party must give direction to intellectuals, teaching them common principles and aligning them with its organizational imperatives and tactical objectives. Gramsci therefore followed other revolutionaries in recommending the model of 'democratic centralism' in the Party: different and opposed viewpoints could be discussed, but when a decision had been made, everyone had to commit to it and dissension thereafter was forbidden (see 1971: 155). That way, the hierarchy proper to revolution (with its militaristic sense of executive command) is maintained alongside the need to hear divergent opinions, ensuring 'continual adaptation of the organisation to the real movement, a matching of thrusts from below with orders from above' (1971: 188). Given its role in absorbing intellectuals from other social classes, who may have different values and allegiances from those of the industrial working class, the Party needed to maintain 'homogeneity between the leadership and the rank and file' (1971: 158). Gramsci's suggestions for the Party's internal functioning combined a Leninist model of revolutionary command with the social democratic model of a mass-based party. These are, doubtless, contradictory imperatives, and getting them to work together at all presupposes general agreement on the Party's basic objectives. Gramsci's image of the Party is, on the one hand, democratically inclined – he was deeply critical of Stalin's efforts to impose bureaucratic control on communist parties – but, on the other hand, potentially authoritarian, especially when he suggests that 'in men's consciences' the Party 'takes the place of the divinity or the categorical imperative' (1971: 133), suggesting it should become a kind of replacement Church with its own religion. This is certainly not a liberal model of democratic participation, as Femia notes (1981: 172; but see also Vacca 2020: ch. 4). For his sympathizers, Gramsci offers a uniquely inclusive and democratic model of radical politics (see Sassoon 1987; Golding 1992). But, for others, hegemonic strategy may seem barely democratic at all. At times, Gramsci's formulations suggest a strong tolerance for disagreement but, equally, he endorses the need for firm discipline, 'total' dedication to the Party, and an intolerance of dissent.

Tensions in Gramsci's Analysis

Gramsci's *Notebooks* are a feast for scholars hunting textual nuances. There are numerous, sometimes slight, variations across his many remarks. Inevitably, then, there are tensions in the positions he explored. We cannot know precisely what he would have made of his own ideas had he survived prison. Would he revise them further to fit with changed circumstances? Might he have adapted them to endorse the prevailing communist line, or even oppose it? These questions are unanswerable. But we can see the conceptual and strategic tensions that later readers of Gramsci have had to confront.

For instance, the boundary between force and consent remains ambiguous. At times, hegemony is identified by Gramsci solely with consent – but hegemonic politics also involves a 'balance' of force *and* consent. At what moment, we might ask, does consent also involve force, and how can it be justified? Is coercion necessary in civil society, too? How much violence is acceptable before any consent becomes – as in the case of Fascism – little more than a smokescreen for systematic bullying and intimidation? Gramsci's later readers have been critical because he tends to juxtapose force and consent, rather than treat them as intertwined aspects of class domination (see, e.g., Anderson 1976–7).

The strategic question that arises here is whether, and to what degree, a socialist revolution requires widespread consent *prior* to seizing state power. Gramsci implied that a moment of violence to ensure a rupture with the old order would be likely. But, elsewhere, he suggests that force need only be minimal, especially if a new hegemony had been prepared. These are not wholly contrary positions, and they suggest that actual historical conditions make a considerable difference. But they invite different tactical approaches for a revolutionary movement: prepare for violence or not? Compromise with adversaries or be ready to defeat them? Not unrealistically, Gramsci presents the achievement of hegemony as a gradual process, yet one that would very likely meet clear limits under capitalism, where property ownership and the control of production are fundamental. Although he spoke of leadership and consent, Gramsci never absolutely relinquished the militaristic tone in his analysis.

Another tension lies in the way Gramsci argued against economism. His emphasis on subjectivity as a complex, independent factor irreducible to economic interests, and his unique attention to popular beliefs and common sense, underscored his view that a Marxist obsession with class was intellectually mistaken and politically damaging. Hegemony implied not simply an alliance of separate classes, differentiated by their structurally derived interests and mechanically conjoined, but, rather, a wholly new collective subject described as 'national popular'.

Yet Gramsci never entirely gave up on class as the necessary foundation of hegemonic politics. Although he insisted that individual subjects are constituted in multiple ways, nonetheless he argues that all ideologies and social experiences are inescapably inflected by the practical (or 'economic') relations of class. That creates a tension within hegemonic leadership: to what extent can a social class transcend its corporate interests to cooperate with allies? How vital is a specifically *class* consciousness to the national-popular hegemony? It remains unclear to what extent hegemony must be the expression of a dominant class, or whether it can function independently.

Finally, as I have noted, Gramsci's account of Party strategy presents an ethical tension between the authority of political leadership and the liberties of those under it. Gramsci is often regarded as a relatively 'liberal' Marxist because he acknowledges and values diversity. But his insistence on ideological and organizational discipline remains in tension with his aspiration for a non-dogmatic, mass-based party with cross-class appeal.

None of these tensions is a devastating flaw. Indeed, in some respects, they underline the subtlety and complexity of Gramsci's arguments, as well as their unfinished character. By recasting hegemony for modern conditions, he intended to confront a messy historical reality he couldn't conceptually resolve away.

Togliatti and the 'New Party'

Gramsci died in April 1937 before he could take up the conditional release belatedly granted by the Fascist authorities. His *Notebooks* were smuggled out of Italy and kept safe until the defeat of Nazism and Fascism in 1945. Few knew anything of their contents until after the war. Had Gramsci survived and the Soviet authorities known of his ideas, he would likely have been silenced like other critics of Stalinism. As well as his dismay at Soviet authoritarianism, Gramsci's undogmatic approach to Marxism, dismissal of crude scientism, and attentiveness to a flexible politics of alliances put him quite at odds with the communist regime. Seclusion in prison had probably saved him and his ideas from being erased entirely from official communist history.

Inevitably, Gramsci's posthumous legacy was shaped by the emerging international context: the 'Cold War' between opposed ideological blocks of states led by the US and the Soviet Union. Vital here was the leadership of Palmiro Togliatti (1893–1964), Gramsci's friend and comrade, who led the PCI after the latter's arrest. It was Togliatti who oversaw the first publication of the *Notebooks*, and it was his reading of Gramsci's ideas, particularly its implications for the direction of the Party, that initiated hegemony's postwar reception (see Gundle 1995).

As leader, Togliatti pursued the line he and Gramsci agreed together in 1926: underscoring the mistake of 'detaching' the Party from the working class, and insisting that strategy be adapted to the 'objective situation' in Italy (Togliatti 1979: 26). That meant promoting cross-class alliances with other anti-Fascists (led by the communists, of course). Fascism, Togliatti argued throughout the 1930s, was not 'something set' – a fixed, homogeneous force – but, rather, a still-developing form of authoritarian politics that had to be resisted (Togliatti 1976: 26–7).

When Togliatti returned to Italy in 1944, he chose, again, to adapt to the new situation, building upon his Party's participation in the 'national liberation'. He announced the PCI's transformation into a 'new party' (*partito nuovo*) that departed from the Bolshevik model by embracing constitutional democracy and political transparency, and engaging national debate over practical issues: 'Our policy is a mass policy; it is, and intends to be, a policy of the people; and the means by which it is translated into practice must be of a mass and popular character' (1979: 31). For him, revolutionary violence simply would not work, especially when US warships were moored off the coast of Italy. Conscious of the Party's vulnerability in the new national and international contexts, but also aware of its surging popularity, Togliatti redeveloped the interwar policy of anti-Fascism for the new conditions of mass democracy (Sassoon 1981).

Ostensibly a Communist Party seeking the overthrow of capitalism, under Togliatti the PCI developed a mass base of loyal supporters. It rooted its organization widely and deeply in Italian society, developing forms of democratic participation that embedded it in popular life, local government, and workplaces, becoming the largest Communist Party in Western Europe (Shore 1990). Notably, it cultivated a strong cultural influence through its Party schools, newspapers, and reviews, permitting its intellectuals considerable leeway in developing their own views and, where possible, dissenting from the Party line. In shaping the Party this way, Togliatti took his cue from Gramsci's prison writings.

Originally, Togliatti defended Gramsci as a home-grown Marxist, loyal to the Russian Revolution. But after the death of Stalin in 1953, and in 1956 when the USSR admitted the Soviet leader's 'cult of personality' and crimes, he shifted his tone (Togliatti 1979: 115–42). Gramsci was affirmed as a unique thinker in his own right, and the concepts of 'hegemony', 'war of position', and the general theory of the Party were presented as his distinctive formulation (1979: 200–6). Togliatti portrayed his pragmatic strategy as a response to Gramsci's thoughts on historical conditions in Italy, which necessitated a gradual process of building socialism by cultivating a cultural and political presence across civil society: 'We have already managed to achieve great advances as a party, and to make the working-class movement and all Italian society move forward by following the teaching of Gramsci. We must be able to return continually to this teaching' (1979: 159). This so-called 'Italian road to socialism' (*via italiana al socialismo*) underscored the primacy of distinctively national conditions. Togliatti attributed to Gramsci the idea of the Party as a 'collective intellectual' – a creative, unifying centre gathering around it civic and cultural forces to unite the working class with the nation (1979: 198–202).

Nonetheless, Togliatti was accused of *doppieza*, or 'duplicity' – not least by the US-aligned Christian Democrat Party, which permanently blocked the communists from national governing coalitions. On the one hand, the communists endorsed representative democracy, respected legal order, public institutions, and multi-party diversity, and were willing to compromise on their 'ultimate' goals. On the other, they stayed true to the legacy (if not the model) of the Russian Revolution, the international leadership of the Soviet Union, and the Marxist tradition that identified social ills with capitalism, advocating its substitution – through 'structural reforms' – with a more participatory democratic socialism. That implied *both* a parliamentary reformism aimed at forging governmental coalitions *and* a revolutionary transformation whereby the Party leads society beyond parliamentary democracy. So, was the Communist Party committed to reform or to revolution? Was it seeking hegemony *within* representative democracy or, rather, to *replace* it?

As we have seen, this is a problem that can be traced – to some extent – to the tensions in Gramsci's own writings. At what moment – if ever – does a consensual war of position become a violent war of manoeuvre? Gramsci believed he was living through an 'organic crisis' of capitalism that made revolution a realistic (if distant) prospect. Togliatti, on the other hand, judged the postwar situation differently. A canny leader, he understood that Gramsci's writings offered important resources for adjusting communist strategy while maintaining a semblance of continuity with the revolutionary aspiration. But the age of catastrophic collapses and revolutionary assaults was, in his view, over – the Party had to work within new, post-Fascist parameters, including parliamentary democracy, while offering a popular vision of socialism that appealed across Italian society. Despite his more radical critics, keeping the Party committed to structural change while also contributing to the stabilization of postwar Italy was no small achievement. As historian Donald Sassoon (1990) underlines: for all its strategic ambiguity (which deprived it of real power) the PCI contributed significantly to embedding Italian democracy.

Conclusion

In formulating hegemony to re-conceptualize revolution, Gramsci transformed it from a narrow principle of leadership into a general theory of how political orders are established and maintained through the management of coercion and consent. Gramsci's legacy is a concept that connects a range of ideas and principles concerning power, strategy, culture, and the prospects for radical social change. There are, as I have suggested, a number of accents and tensions in his thought that support different ways of interpreting and 'applying' hegemony. That is why it might be better to think of Gramsci as an innovator who offers ways of posing questions about power and domination through hegemony – recognizing the spectrum of possibilities it opens up – rather than providing final answers.

The interwar European situation out of which Gramsci's ideas emerged was a very particular one, characterized by institutional crisis, radical ideological shifts and re-alignments, and profound political violence. After the Second World War, the mass politics that Gramsci was only beginning to understand came substantially to define western capitalist democracies. In that new context (which Togliatti had to confront), politics was conducted in circumstances largely of institutional stability, polarized but homogeneous ideological division, and relative national and international peace. The topic of revolutionary strategy became, gradually, less urgent than the question of how to understand the character and mechanisms of domination in these new conditions. Strategic questions still remained, but the opportunities for radicals and revolutionaries were increasingly constrained – not by violent, anti-democratic dictatorships, but by relatively popular, democratic institutions, redistributive welfare states, and inclusive political cultures. As we will see in the next chapter, Gramsci's formulation of hegemony helped to stimulate a rigorous re-examination by Marxists of postwar capitalist states.

3
Marxism: Hegemony and the State

The transformation of western states after the war into major providers of welfare and, more generally, the cultural and political effects of postwar 'consumer capitalism' provided a whole new context to the discussion about hegemony. More than just a remnant of revolutionary jargon, in this period 'hegemony' became a term of art for radical social and political analysis. It fed into academic social science, particularly among political sociologists and cultural analysts, to help to explain new modes of domination in 'developed capitalism'.

For a while, capitalist states exhibited considerable degrees of popular consent, with full employment and increasing affluence. Postwar economies enjoyed a period of remarkable growth, which materially improved the lives of swathes of working people, enabling greater health, education, and social mobility for many citizens. While inequalities remained and social conflicts persisted, western states nonetheless appeared, for a while, to have achieved degrees of social integration and political stability unimaginable in the interwar years (Judt 2005: 242). By the mid-1960s, however, those achievements began to fray, as domestic growth declined and processes of decolonization shook the assumed preeminence of Anglo-American culture.

For young Marxists and radical critics, hegemony offered a way to understand the capitalist state as an evolving political and cultural formation. Gramsci was increasingly acknowledged as a distinctly 'western' Marxist, focused, like others in that tradition, on specifically ideological and political dimensions of class domination (Anderson 1979). His writings on hegemony offered concepts aimed uniquely at political dynamics – its shifts and reversals, patterns and variations – rather than fixed principles or dogmatic claims. As we'll see, this proved significant for those looking to reconnect Marxian accounts of capitalism to the specificities of history and politics. Yet, in emphasizing cultural and political conditions, hegemony also problematized the Marxist assumption of the 'primacy' of economic relations in social change.

Consensus Politics?

What prompted the revival of hegemony in the 1960s? In part, it was a response to the contrast between new forms of social conflict and the inadequacies of the theoretical inheritance of Marxism. Transformations in the organization of states gradually resolved many of the deepest inequalities that had assailed prewar societies: extensive forms of welfare (particularly in health, housing, and education), full employment, unprecedented economic growth, and new opportunities for people to consume and to enjoy leisure all diminished many of the class-based conflicts of the interwar years.

In western Europe and America, the state was less and less a distant, authoritarian structure ruling by force, and more a collection of public agencies that coordinated (and, in some instances, actually owned and ran) public services, democratically represented all citizens and sought to manage the interests of both capital and labour, and taxed and redistributed wealth. Western societies came to exhibit a substantial degree of consensus, at least at an elite level, over basic values and the function of political power in the postwar era (see Kavanagh 1994). For mainstream political scientists, that was taken as a sign of satisfaction among citizens with the general orientation of governments and their ruling elites, signalling an end to the ideological polarization that defined the interwar years. Class conflict and destabilizing political hostilities were, to a great extent, perceived as 'exhausted' (Almond and Verba 1965; Bell 2000).

But new forms of division did emerge – around, for example, the atomic bomb and the threat of nuclear armageddon, around racism and black civil rights in the US, processes of decolonization as former imperial holdings achieved independence, and localized military conflagrations (such as the Vietnam war). These conflicts – which had many histories, aims, and actors – could not easily be bundled into the binary logic of class struggle. In addition to a growing 'counter-cultural' suspicion of stultifying corporate capitalism and bureaucratic government, they signalled fractures in the supposedly harmonious postwar consensus. As the authors of the *May Day Manifesto* put it in 1968: 'The political aim of the new capitalism ... is to muffle real conflict, to dissolve it into a false political consensus; to build, not a genuine and radical community of life and interest, but a bogus conviviality between every social group' (Williams 1968: 143). Such suspicion fed into the expansion of 'new social movements' through the late 1960s and 1970s. As economic growth began to slow and class conflicts erupted, a wider sense of cultural crisis in affluent social democracies of the West solidified.

Marxist political thinking after the war was, initially, rather underdeveloped. Cold War polarization had resulted in political marginalization for European communist parties, and new thinking was often discouraged in favour of rigid, Soviet-led orthodoxy. Marxists initially had little in the way of intellectual resources to understand the new context. Approaches to the state, politics, and ideology tended to be reductive and instrumentalist (Miliband 1977). State power was still viewed as largely coercive – part of a 'total' economic structure to sustain capitalism. That position had little new to say about postwar social democracy and emerging forms of social conflict. Soon, however, new generations of independent Marxist thinkers arrived – particularly following the death of Stalin in 1953 and the subsequent revelation of his crimes – to challenge both communist orthodoxy and the liberal-conservative mainstream in political science. From the mid-1950s in the UK, the so-called 'New Left' began to draw on Gramsci's ideas to explore the different modalities of state power and to interrogate critically the conditions of cultural and political consensus (Kenny 1995).

Class Consciousness and Elite Culture

A key resource for any discussion of hegemony in the early 1960s was the journal *New Left Review*, especially the analyses set out by its then editors, Marxist historians Perry Anderson and Tom Nairn (see Nairn 1981; Anderson 1992). In what came to be known as the 'Anderson–Nairn theses', the authors explored (in separate but complementary enquiries) the historical formation of the British state and its emerging post-imperial crises.

Anderson and Nairn traced the weaknesses of the postwar British state to its compromised bourgeois revolution in the seventeenth century (Nairn 1981: 11–91; Anderson 1992: 15–47). Rather than a revolution in which one class replaced another, with its own cultural and political project, 'capitalist hegemony', they argued, had been achieved through a conflict within, not against, the rural landowning class. Agrarian capitalism had created the conditions for later industrial expansion. But its legacy was not a modernizing social force with an independent 'class consciousness'. Rather, as Anderson put it, the bourgeoisie remained culturally subservient, 'bent on integrating itself into the aristocracy' (1992: 21), unable to project itself as a wholesale break with the past. Sheltered beneath the cultural prestige of a class whose traditions (such as its schooling and universities) it uncritically endorsed, the British bourgeoisie never proclaimed its own ideological programme but remained 'diffused in a miasma of commonplace prejudices and taboos' (1992: 31).

Consequently, without a modernizing bourgeoisie to define itself against, the working class was unable satisfactorily to project its interests beyond particularistic 'guild' traditions, resulting in a long-standing attachment to 'labourism' – the defence of the separate, corporate interests of workers, and not an ambitious project of socialism. Consequently, the creaking British state clung to the hegemony of social conventions and structures of an elitist and patrician imperial order, with a working class that failed 'to set and impose goals for society as a whole' (1992: 33). With the retreat of Empire, the British ruling class, argued Anderson and Nairn, became increasingly backward-looking and uninterested in technological or scientific advances that might revive its fortunes. The result, by the 1960s, was the lacklustre Macmillan government and the foreign policy disaster of the Suez crisis.

Anderson's and Nairn's analyses focused in large part on the presence in the British state of a narrow 'establishment': the ruling elite, with a conservative proclivity for 'high' culture, shallow obsession with 'intellectual heritage' over innovation (Anderson 1992: 48), and a curious 'faith in the mystique' of its insular, inter-class system of compromise over any radical or popular-based affiliations (Nairn 1981: 43). In these analyses, hegemony functioned principally as a model of cultural state-building, foregrounding class consciousness, intellectual leadership, and the generation of a broad, popular alliance – a model against which the British experience fell substantially short. Anderson himself later confessed that this early approach was overly preoccupied with culture. It assumed, perhaps like Gramsci himself, that the French Revolution was the template for a 'proper' bourgeois state – a new ruling class making a concerted break with the past, and committed to a modern, republican style of government. But, we might ask, why should the French Revolution assume this role?

The elite culture perspective on hegemony shifted Marxist political analysis onto notably Gramscian themes. But it also mirrored the preoccupations of the time among other radical political analysts, who understood political power in terms of alliances and shared values among restricted social groups working inside public institutions (see Miliband 1973; Mills 2000). Anderson and Nairn offered a critical, historically focused version of that approach, reinforcing a prevalent perception of the British state as encumbered by an anachronistic ruling elite with a narrow social base of support. This punctured the view of there being a natural political consensus and, in its stead, foregrounded the historical compromises and limitations of a restricted hegemonic leadership.

Structuralism and the Capitalist State

The structuralist tendency in Marxist theory emerged in the 1960s under the leadership of French philosopher Louis Althusser. Structuralists in various fields claimed that social action and individual choices are explained not by conscious decisions but by fundamental organizing principles (or structures) that order their relations. Althusser also sought to revive Marxist theory, not as a form of historical enquiry but, rather, as an independent 'science' of the 'structural ensemble' known as the 'mode of production' (Althusser 1969; Althusser and Balibar 1970). The capitalist mode of production comprised a set of economic relations (based on private property), which allocated places and functions to other, 'relatively autonomous' structures such as ideology and politics. A properly Marxist critique of capitalism, Althusser argued, consisted in understanding how these levels interacted with each other, *not* in attributing power and domination to historical agents who disseminate beliefs. Individuals and social classes, for structuralists, were mere 'bearers' of the structural roles allocated to them, not their authors. Marx's insights were presented as a form of 'theoretical anti-humanism' (Althusser 1969: 229–31) – capitalist power and domination were not 'willed' into existence, but structured relations that transcended beliefs.

Althusser's philosophy had a transformative effect on Continental Marxist thought (Elliott 1987). It promised the reinvention of Marxism as a revolutionary science to analyse 'objective' conditions across various contexts, rather than interpret 'phenomenological' perceptions and experiences. Against the dogmas of the Soviet Union, it also offered a nuanced approach to class politics and strategy that rejected reductionism and economic determinism. Class interests, political affiliations, and the ideals to which they subscribe are not 'expressions' of a single underlying economic structure; they are the outcome of combined, or 'overdetermined', structural levels. Sectors of the industrial working class, for example, could simultaneously be positioned economically as workers, ideologically as Catholics, and politically as anti-Fascists. Indeed, for Althusser, ideology described the way subjects merely 'imagined' their relationship to the real conditions of their existence (Althusser 1971: 153). With its own internal associations and logic, ideology's connection to class only ever came in the 'last instance' – as an effect of the mode of production on the 'totality'. Nonetheless, he continued, under capitalism, subjects were typically captured by a 'dominant ideology' disseminated through 'ideological state apparatuses' – formal and informal institutions, such as the education system – that misdirected workers from the reality of their exploitation. In Althusser's Marxism, then, politics and culture were complex formations that intersected in a constantly moving ensemble, whose dynamics and permutations had to be mapped and analysed.

How did structuralism contribute to the analysis of the state and hegemony? The work of political sociologist Nicos Poulantzas was vital in applying structuralist insights to politics (see Poulantzas 1973, 2008). Poulantzas, a Greek-born Marxist resident in Paris, insisted that, structurally speaking, the state was a 'capitalist state', not 'a state *in* capitalist society'. It was not a neutral instrument, occasionally steered by specific classes. Rather, the state was positioned within the capitalist mode of production as a 'relatively autonomous' level, 'formally' independent from economic relations but subject to their overall determination. That permitted it to operate as a disinterested arbiter, at a distance from any one class.

For Poulantzas, the state functions as 'a factor of cohesion', a site from which to project unifying ideologies of the 'general interest' while, at the same time, servicing the mode of production by maintaining its general conditions (such as property relations, the subservience of labour to capital, and so on). Of course, political parties and other social forces (representing separate 'class fractions') compete to command or influence the state apparatus at any specific moment, but its formal autonomy meant class bias was a structural feature, not a consequence of its personnel. There, argued Poulantzas (2008: 120–38), lay the theoretical error of Anderson's and Nairn's arguments – thinking that the British state's failings derived from its ruling class's lack of class consciousness and weak control over its apparatuses. Poulantzas made a similar, well-known protest against 'empirical' Marxist theories of the state, such as that of Ralph Miliband (1973), which emphasized the personal affiliations and shared values of political and economic elites (2008: 172–85, 270–93). The structural position of the state meant that it was not necessary for the bourgeoisie itself to command political power in order to be the dominant class.

Poulantzas's theory of the capitalist state sought a more rigorous understanding of hegemony than the historical account given by Marxist historians. Rather than a subjective ideal, hegemony described a precise configuration of bourgeois class fractions that, at any specific phase or conjuncture, unified around an account of the general interest (1973: 137–41). Together, these fractions formed a 'power bloc' that condensed their otherwise contradictory interests and imposed general strategic direction on state apparatuses (1973: 229–45). More sensitive to concrete variations than most structuralists, Poulantzas undertook analyses of different permutations of the capitalist state – 'normal' states were organized with a power bloc led by a dominant fraction, such as industrial or financial capital; and 'exceptional' forms of state, such as those of interwar Fascism, relied on dictatorships because there was no dominant fraction to lead them. Italian Fascism and German Nazism, for example, utilized the relative autonomy of the state to mediate fractions of the petty bourgeoisie, landed capital, and monopoly capital (Poulantzas 1974). In his later work, Poulantzas began to look at what he called 'authoritarian statist' strategies that corresponded to the contemporary crisis of the postwar power bloc and the emerging dominance of international capital (Poulantzas 1978).

'Hegemony', for Poulantzas, was principally a term to explore how capitalists politically organized their common interests through the state. In rejecting an emphasis on ideas and experiences, he highlighted instead the shifting blocs of class forces underpinning regime types. In this, he undoubtedly brought a theoretical rigour and nuance to the analysis of hegemony. Yet, like structuralist Marxism in general, his highly theoretical approach seemed inclined to functionalism – that is, attributing to capitalism a capacity for self-reproduction by assimilating division and conflict (despite his own regular emphasis on 'contradictions' and class struggles). If hegemony always services the dominant class fraction, then what difference does it really make who controls it? Moreover, if the mode of production determines everything 'in the last instance', how independent could politics and ideology ever be from economic structures?

Although Poulantzas gradually softened his structuralism, he did not closely explore how bourgeois hegemony might also appeal to working classes, nor did he consider how it may apply to a revolutionary strategy for the left (see 1973: 204). Indeed, his analysis of the dynamics of ideology (its subjective appeal to different classes or to non-class movements) remained underdeveloped. Insisting on the 'objective' dimensions of hegemony severely limited the extent to which structuralist Marxism could illuminate innovations and transformations in politics (see Laclau 1977: 51–79).

A Dialectic of Structure and Strategy?

With structuralist Marxism, hegemony gained conceptual sophistication but lost its ease of use as a measure of concrete politics. Yet that dynamism – shifting alliances and ideological innovations – became increasingly salient as social democratic governments sought to resolve economic and political crises in the 1970s and 1980s. A more flexible research programme, drawn from the insights of Poulantzas's later thinking, was supplied by British Marxist sociologist Bob Jessop (1990). In Jessop's formulation, the state is conceived as itself a political strategy, combining *both* structural and strategic dimensions.

The capitalist state, Jessop argues, is 'the site, the generator and the product of strategies' to organize capitalism (1990: 260). The institutional separation of legal/political from economic power, as Poulantzas argued, compels different class fractions to coalesce around a general model of economic growth – or what Jessop calls an 'accumulation strategy', corresponding broadly to the interests of the leading fraction (1990: 198–206). Connected to accumulation strategies (but not equivalent to them) are 'hegemonic projects', which Jessop understands as political and cultural alliances that formulate accumulation strategies in wider, non-economic terms – that is, as civil programmes to unify allies and isolate rivals (1990: 207–15). As well as being directed *at* states, accumulation strategies and hegemonic projects are, together, 'political strategies' elaborated *through* states. They articulate public authority with 'the economy' through forms of intervention, coordinating and managing the operation of public agencies, and pursuing policy initiatives. Finally, successful political strategies materially transform the state, adjusting its relations to society by privileging certain capacities and social forces, and diminishing others. As a consequence, the state is 'strategically selective', amenable more to certain options than to others, as a result of previous strategic choices. This generates constraints and opportunities for subsequent political strategies (1990: 260–2).

In Jessop's 'strategic-relational' approach, the capitalist state is the locus of a 'complex dialectic between structures and strategies' (1990: 267). The state's structural separation from economic interests makes possible, but never guarantees, capitalism's reproduction. Unlike structuralist Marxists, Jessop found a way to conceptualize the relation between the state and capitalism without insisting on determination 'in the last instance'. He introduced a considerable degree of contingency, underscoring especially the capitalist state's strategic openness to revision and reversal. That enhanced the importance of hegemony as the dynamic component in how class political strategies were organized, without making the entire state depend on it or limiting its reach to the dominant classes only. An accumulation strategy might be delivered through a variety of different hegemonic projects over time, depending on the political conjuncture. Hegemonic alliances and ideologies may recruit more or less widely across the population, expanding or reforming as accumulation strategies are elaborated and transform the circumstances. As we shall see, these nuances became significant in Jessop's analysis of Thatcherism.

Popular Culture, Ideology, and Crisis

Hegemony also helped to unlock critical appreciation of 'culture' in postwar societies. Like the idea of the state, cultural practices had traditionally been understood by Marxists either to be irrelevant to the class struggle or to overlap directly with the interests of classes. In the postwar era, however, culture became a key site of many of the tensions and conflicts brought by Fordist industrial relations and consumer capitalism. On the one hand, states increasingly justified themselves as integrated communities with common 'national cultures', aligned to the 'West'. On the other, mass culture and commercial leisure pursuits disrupted traditional, often 'elite', cultural references and the hierarchies maintained through them. For certain New Left thinkers, hegemony directed attention to the shifting boundaries of popular cultural tastes and the wider ideological struggles they articulated.

In the UK, what later came to be known as the discipline of cultural studies contributed significantly to radical social and political enquiry. Early New Left intellectuals were especially interested in workers' education, 'popular' history, and the contribution to democratic life of the British labour movement, which they saw as the basis for a 'bottom up' form of socialist politics (Gilbert 2008: 11–14). These figures – including E. P. Thompson, Raymond Williams, and Stuart Hall – were sympathetic to the ways working people, rather than elites, experienced and managed their subordination. This led to interest in the collective pastimes of ordinary people, rather than traditional, 'high' culture of the elite: popular entertainment like football or television, rather than opera or literary classics. Out of their enquiries emerged a distinct strand of 'cultural Marxism' born of an attraction to collective struggles 'from below', not theoretical abstraction or strict ideological alignment (Dworkin 1997).

Williams and Hall were, in different ways, attuned to questions of how people themselves made sense of their own experience, how they participated in forms of play and leisure, and thereby 'negotiated' their experiences of social subordination (for example, at school and work, as well as to public authority). The public emergence of the 'teenager' (as compulsory school attendance delayed full adulthood), the expansion of leisure time brought by full employment, but also greater literacy and the ability to invest in styles of dress, domestic goods, music, and other symbolic objects that registered taste and distinction – all began in the late 1950s to call into question the received, class- and elite-based division of taste into 'high' and 'low' forms. 'Culture' was increasingly understood as the medium for working people to judge and enjoy things of value, not only prestigious intellectual or artistic pursuits. Participation in this popular culture involved encounters with, even resistance to, socially dominant values and beliefs – or hegemony.

'Culture is ordinary', declared Williams, and a 'common culture' was constantly evolving through 'active debate and amendment through the pressures of experience', not something handed down ready-made from on high (Williams 2001: 11). As the name for an ongoing dispute over what is 'common', Williams argued later, hegemony was never a homogeneous, 'dominant ideology' owned exclusively by one class and imposed on ordinary people, but, rather, 'a whole body of practices and expectations, over the whole of living: our senses and assignments of energy, our shaping perceptions of ourselves and our world'. Independent of any one social group, culture signalled the moving boundary between domination and subordination – between a 'social lived process' and 'dominant meanings and values' (Williams 1977: 109). Rather than cementing an otherwise solid structure, then, cultural hegemony described a dynamic, ongoing process of sharing, selecting, approving, and disapproving of purportedly common symbols and values. It demonstrated that working people, unequal and oppressed as they were, nonetheless actively negotiated the subjective experience of their subordination (Williams 1977). Social domination was experienced through what Williams (1961: 64) called a 'structure of feeling', not just in the objective political strategies of organized movements, parties, and elites.

The leading advocate of a cultural Marxist approach to hegemony was Jamaican-born scholar Stuart Hall, one of the early founders of the New Left and a major influence on British cultural studies (see Hall 1988). Unlike Williams, whose 'expressive' approach viewed culture as an evolving whole, Hall was particularly attuned to the fractures in postwar cultural experience and to a creeping sense of cultural crisis in the UK, especially after the May 1968 student revolts had failed to bring the left substantial political gains (Gilbert 2008: 24–7). Hall was especially receptive to developments in Continental thought, and willing to apply these to modern, urban cultural experience. Taking up leadership of the Centre for Contemporary Cultural Studies (CCCS) at the University of Birmingham, in the 1970s he oversaw a variety of innovative projects exploring working-class culture – on youth sub-cultures, magazine reading, football hooliganism, media analysis, and television viewing – and utilizing new ethnographic and semiotic methods (see Hall and Jefferson 1975; CCCS 1977). These projects were attentive to the immediate ideological and political context, which increasingly obsessed over youth, law and order, and, in particular, race and immigration as markers of a larger anxiety over national 'decline'.

Hall and his co-researchers drew on the work of Althusser, Poulantzas, and especially Gramsci to explore the peculiar cultural symptoms of an evolving 'narrative' of crisis. In texts such as *Policing the Crisis* (Hall et al. 1978), for example, the clustering of hysterical media reports on young black men's involvement in mugging was examined as an instance of the 'conjunctural crisis' of the British state. The decline of ruling-class hegemony, they argued, was manifest ideologically in 'moral panics' over national cultural integrity, crime, and race – a point underlined by the rise of far-right racist politics in the UK and the efforts to take advantage of it by mainstream politicians, such as Enoch Powell MP. Public anxieties were thus read as complex, mediating forms in the fracturing of the postwar settlement on which social consensus had been built. Again, hegemony was understood here as the more or less stable horizon of popular beliefs, values, and norms concerning the family, social order, and personal success through which different classes and groups had compromised in the postwar years. Hall and his colleagues focused on how this settlement – and the dynamics of its crisis – was produced and disseminated at a ground level, or ideologically.

Hall himself developed a distinctive and complex understanding of ideology as a field comprising class and non-class (or 'popular') elements. Ideology, as Gramsci uniquely understood, was a wide and flexible terrain of contest, where the 'class-pertinence' of ideas and beliefs (concerning crime or youth, for example) was achieved not via anonymous structures working behind the scenes but by symbolic interventions that inflected them with wider, metaphorical significance (Hall et al. 1977; Hall 1986). Crises in economic and political governance were thus presented and experienced as moral crises concerning the integrity of the people. Indeed, as we'll see below, populism – the appeal to an image of the people, rather than class – became a common point of reference in the late 1970s for Marxists looking to understand the dynamics of the political conjuncture (see Laclau 1977: 143–98).

Hall's approach to hegemony brought together both the cultural and the structural dimensions of the concept. He combined a view of a hegemonic order as a complex domain of lived experience with an appreciation of the institutionalized class interests and ideologies to which popular experience was articulated. But Hall also understood the state as a precarious balance of ideological and political forces whose consensual basis was always under construction, and increasingly in crisis. Exploring hegemony involved, for him, tracing a perpetually moving target – not a fixed edifice of structured interests but a lively, contested stream of statements, sentiments, and behaviours that irrupted into life as questions around a common culture.

Rebuilding Consent: from Thatcherism to Populism

I've presented the Marxian approaches to hegemony in terms of two branches. This is a simplified picture, of course, and we should beware of overstating it – Marxian analyses of hegemony overlapped and developed in response to each other and to ongoing events. Both branches registered the complexity of politics and ideology in postwar capitalism and sought to be attentive to the unique conditions of the 'conjuncture'. Nonetheless, the distinction captures their different preoccupations. The structural branch conceived hegemony as inseparable from institutional arrangements and class economic forces, while the cultural branch conceived it as an ongoing ideological contest. Together, however, they offer rich theoretical insights for analysing how states and national cultures form a strategic field for rebuilding the social bases of consent during periods of social and economic change.

One of the most instructive examples in this regard is the phenomenon of 'Thatcherism' – the political ideas and programme of the governments led, initially, by Margaret Thatcher in the UK, from 1979 through to the late 1990s. In promoting a break with the postwar social democratic consensus, Thatcher took a radical stand against the notion of the state as a provider of welfare and as an intervenor in the economy. Responding to the economic stagnation and governmental crises of the 1970s, she shifted her party's programme to an aggressive attack on the postwar settlement, blaming a generic 'socialism' for the ills of industrial decline and societal disarray. In its place, she argued for free markets, a tough, minimal state, and a society based on individual responsibility and 'family values'. In tune with the adminis- trations of Ronald Reagan in the US, Thatcher's governments sought a wholesale shake-up in the state's relation to society. Hers was both an institutional and an ideological project, aimed at a new settlement combining free markets with a strong state (Gamble 1994). It involved reorganizing the public function of the state – deregulating, privatizing, and allowing the market to determine success – and polarizing politics by relentless hostility to critics, opponents, and a host of perceived threats to social order. Despite its evident divisiveness (indeed, because of it), it was also a surprisingly popular project, securing the Conservative Party a record four terms of office.

In what sense was Thatcherism a *hegemonic* project? Not all Marxists subscribed to that characterization. For some, it was merely an intensified version of class politics: an attack on the working class by an anti-socialist right-wing government (see Miliband et al. 1987). But, for Gramscians such as Hall and Jessop, it was a strategy to lead society in a particular direction. The term 'Thatcherism' was itself coined by Hall and Martin Jacques, editors of the magazine *Marxism Today*, to signal that effort to impose a new trajectory on the state by fashioning a new consensus (Hall and Jacques 1983). Hall interpreted Thatcherism primarily as an ideological project, aimed at transforming popular 'common sense'. Jessop, on the other hand, understood it as a state strategy directed principally at delivering a new project of accumulation.

Hall's reading of Thatcherism built upon his earlier analyses of the media, popular culture, and crisis in British society (Hall 1988). Thatcherism was defined not wholly by economic or social policies, but by a worldview that challenged the constellation of ideas, conventions, and policies of postwar social democracy. This was evident in the way it appealed to common-sense values of hard work, individual responsibility, and the primacy of the family as the basis of social order.

> Thatcherism discovered a powerful means of translating economic doctrine into the language of experience, moral imperative and common sense, thus providing a 'philosophy' in the broader sense – an alternative *ethic* to that of the 'caring society'. This translation of a theoretical *ideology* into a populist *idiom* was a major political achievement: and the conversion of hard-faced economics into the language of compulsive *moralism* was, in many ways, the centrepiece of this transformation. (Hall 1988: 47; italics in the original)

In pitting these values against the 'self-interest' of trade unions, the incentive-destroying habits of nationalized industries, and the bureaucratic inefficiency of the state, Thatcher offered a provocative 'repertoire' of ideas that Hall, adapting the insights of Poulantzas, described as 'authoritarian populism' (Hall 1988: 123–49). It was an innovative ideological project aimed at rallying not just voters, but all society, around a decisive rupture with the past. The repertoire worked by taking popular experiences of disillusion with social democracy (in industrial relations, education, urban crime) and connecting them to a powerful narrative of social disintegration that demanded urgent repair through firm leadership. The response to Thatcher by the left – both the 'labourist' variety represented by the Labour Party and that of its far-left critics – was, argued Hall, wholly inadequate. In dismissing it as deranged or merely another form of the class war, they failed to grasp Thatcherism's novelty, its popularity, and the scope of its strategic ambitions. As a hegemonic project, Thatcherism was 'a radically novel political formation' (1988: 83) aimed at building a new cultural consensus (Hall and Jacques 1983).

Hall characterized Thatcherism in its early phases as an authoritarian project. He emphasized its appeal to 'law and order', with all the reactionary, criminalizing, and often racialized undertones that phrase carried. In the early 1980s, Thatcher's governments confronted trade unions by using both legal and coercive measures (e.g. against the miners, who were defeated in 1984–5), dealt forcibly with urban unrest and international conflict (e.g. the Falklands war), and presided with callous disregard over historically high unemployment. But, by the mid-1980s, Hall recognized that the authoritarian dimension had diminished in favour of a more positive and popular vision of an entrepreneurial society. Even if it was never fully hegemonic, nonetheless Thatcherism's aspiration to hegemony meant it remained the 'leading force in British political life' (1988: 91). The success of the Thatcher governments led Hall to emphasize the idiom – or 'social imaginary' – through which Thatcherism managed 'to address the fears, the anxieties, the lost identities, of a people' (1988: 167). That capacity to operate through 'collective fantasies', to respond to popular lived experience by directing it towards often contradictory aspirations (such as greater individual freedom alongside a conservative morality of 'family values') was the mark of its appeal.

By contrast, Jessop and his co-authors' reading of Thatcherism stressed the economic and institutional dimensions of hegemony (see Jessop et al. 1984, 1988). Ideology was certainly important and Jessop et al. acknowledged Hall's contribution. But they also accused him of 'ideologism', or overstating the significance of ideology in Thatcherism, obscuring its ambiguities, and confusion as to whether its authoritarianism was 'exceptional' or a permanent feature of

its politics. For them, Hall had conceived hegemony exclusively in discursive terms, giving insufficient attention to
the 'structural underpinnings of Thatcherism'. His interpretation generated 'an excessive concern with the mass media
and ideological production at the expense of political and
economic organization' (1984: 37). As such, he endowed
Thatcherism with 'an excessively unified image' that failed to
distinguish its support bases, the different ways it appealed to
them, and the 'internal cleavages' in its alliance.

In their reading, Jessop et al. underscored the relative
continuity of Thatcher governments with their predecessors.
The 'social democratic' consensus was never a coherent
settlement without contradiction, and Thatcherism neither
fully broke with it nor established a new consensus in its
place. Indeed, its governments proceeded more pragmatically than the ideological interpretation suggests, adapting to
conditions as they changed, altering course when necessary,
and reliant on luck as much as intention. Thatcherism
responded not simply to its own ideological narrative, but
also to conjunctural crises in the postwar state's capacity to
manage capitalism and to ensure democratic validity to its
programme. Its authoritarian dimensions were less intrinsic
features than elements of a wider, 'two-nations' strategy that
divided society into productive and 'parasitic' sectors of the
economy. Although it aimed to restructure the state, it had
not established a new 'power bloc'. It relied on financial and
industrial capital but was not fully supported by either, and
there remained tensions in, and popular resistance to, its
strategy. Thus, they concluded, as a project to re-organize
the state, 'Tory hegemony is by no means consolidated'
(1984: 53).

Although they clearly shared common ground, Hall
and Jessop et al. were asking different questions through
hegemony. Hall asked principally about the ideological
'story' at work in Thatcherism, as he highlighted in his
defence (1988: 150–60). Jessop asked about the evolving
economic and institutional conditions to which Thatcherism
responded, and that it sought to transform. These preoccupations reflected different time-scales in their analyses, but
also competing views of the left's priorities: for Hall, a new
cultural narrative; for Jessop, a nuanced Marxist analysis

of political economy. To the chagrin of some (see, e.g., Harris 1992), that eventually led to distinct types of enquiry: cultural studies exploring forms of popular consumption and cultural identity construction, and Marxian state theory investigating the emergent economic and political architectures of 'neo-liberal' capitalism (Brenner and Theodore 2002; Brenner 2004). But their different viewpoints are probably better understood as complementary than as alternatives. Later political analysts have often chosen to combine them by treating hegemonic contests as the interweaving of discursive, economic, and institutional strategies to rebuild and manage the social basis of domestic consent (see Gamble 1994; Hay 1996; Torfing 1998).

Beyond the analysis of Thatcherism, that general approach to hegemony has proved fruitful for understanding the cultural and political dynamics in numerous states undergoing social and economic change (see Davies 1999; Salem 2020). At certain moments, coalitions of social forces, the common-sense ideas and popular beliefs, and techniques and instruments of rule all come into crisis and must adjust to new conditions. Hegemonic analysis examines how the overall *integration* of those different layers – rather than just one in isolation – becomes the object of political strategies. It is visible in once-established beliefs being publicly contested or reinvented to narrate a new situation; in cultural motifs and media technologies mobilized to recruit support; in institutional arrangements and elites being criticized in the name of an all-embracing grievance; and new groups or personalities entering the public realm, posing as representatives of neglected popular demands.

Such interventions are especially evident in contemporary populist politics. Populism, as Hall and Ernesto Laclau (1977) were among the earliest to acknowledge, involves a powerful, elastic appeal to 'the people' and popular feelings in order to disrupt established forms of elite rule and to mobilize disaffected groups and classes behind an individual leader. Populist strategies are often associated with Latin American states – such as Argentina under Juan Perón in the 1940s or, more recently, Venezuela under Hugo Chávez – where weak and corrupt institutions prevent effective interest representation. By mobilizing mass, cross-class support from rural and urban workers, indigenous movements, and intellectuals, populism has long been an effective means to drive institutional change. By deploying a 'myth' of the people, conceived as an autonomous living force within the state (see Rowe and Schelling 1991: 151–92), it selectively condenses various discontents into a general opposition to purported national 'enemies' (de la Torre 2018). Blurring established divisions between 'left' and 'right', populists evade association with 'normal' politics and exploit crises to take aim at the political order, or regime, as such (Moffitt 2015), thereby opening up a potentially hegemonic opportunity to refigure the economy and state.

In its contemporary forms, populism is also used to describe a range of right-wing strategies in the capitalist democracies of the Global North, especially since the financial crisis of 2008. These contest elite consensus, obsessing particularly over immigration, global free markets, or a sense of lost national 'sovereignty' (Moffitt 2020). If they lack Thatcherism's broad appeal, nonetheless they seek a similar rupture with the accepted role and function of government.

For example, the Trump administration in the US from 2017 to 2021 involved just such a popular mobilization. Donald Trump – a millionaire businessman with a profile amplified by 'reality TV' – articulated various grievances against political elites and a 'liberal' consensus over free trade and US global leadership, all perceived as damaging to 'ordinary' Americans. Promising to 'drain the swamp' of special interests, he held regular rallies with his enthusiastic support base to reaffirm his status as a leader untainted by connection to the Washington 'establishment'; and he sought to govern robustly through a vulgar, autocratic style of politics that persistently targeted enemies inside the US (such as immigrants) and outside (such as China). This strategy brought Trump substantial cross-class support and sustained media attention, particularly via Fox News and his personal Twitter feed, generating a powerful image of him directly addressing voters' sense of economic insecurity.

But was it hegemonic? Arguably, Trump only hastened the gradual withdrawal from international leadership that formerly defined postwar US politics (see Stokes 2018). Subsequent administrations will certainly have to work with the lasting consequences of his abrupt and damaging foreign policy decisions, tax cuts, and Supreme Court appointments, as well as the intense resentment of right-wing and white supremacist supporters to which he gave legitimacy. But his administration was notoriously chaotic and divisive, rather than constructive of a stable consensus. Although he deeply polarized politics and successfully transformed the Republican Party into a vehicle for his personal leadership, so far Trump has enjoyed neither the strategic temperament nor resources to reshape popular common sense, or fundamentally to alter the architecture of the US economy.

This example underlines the difficulty of institutionalizing hegemony such that other administrations will endorse a new consensus and work within its parameters. For both Hall and Jessop, by contrast, Thatcherism *did* eventually redefine the cultural and institutional landscape of British politics (Jessop 2015). The subsequent Labour governments of Tony Blair, as a consequence, were regarded by both as fundamentally subservient to the free market ideology and institutional conditions bequeathed by Thatcher (Hall 1998; Jessop 2007).

Conclusion

Hegemony offered postwar Marxists and left radicals a way to analyse politics and ideology in developed capitalist states where consensus, rather than coercion, was broadly the norm. Political and cultural phenomena could be understood as complex, mediating components of societal leadership with their own dynamics, and not mere 'superstructures' transmitting class interests from the 'economic base'. This Gramscian conception developed into a fruitful resource for exploring the unsteady transformations and readjustments of states and national cultures around themes such as race, class, and gender (see Przybylowicz 1990; Gilroy 1992; Artz and Murphy 2000; Connell and Messerschmidt 2005). More than just a label for tactical alliances, hegemony was understood as the dynamic factor that confers degrees of cohesion and stability on society. Yet, as we have seen, among

Marxists there were substantial differences of emphasis about which dimensions of hegemonic leadership were decisive.

As well as focusing on the dynamics of politics and ideology, debates about hegemony and the state – beneath the surface – channelled a growing concern with the status of Marxism as the intellectual and ideological foundation to radical politics. Hegemony's attention to the 'concrete conjuncture' and the contingent 'relations of force' brought into question Marxism's automatic assumption that society was an integrated 'totality' governed by a determining economic logic. It also diminished the privilege given to classes as the primary agents of political struggles. Without discarding the framework of Marxism altogether, analyses of hegemony and the state underscored how actual capitalist societies frequently *diverged* from traditional Marxist expectations. In the next chapter, we'll see how this critical aspect served as the basis to a 'Post-Marxist' reinvention of hegemony.

4
Post-Marxism: Hegemony and Radical Democracy

Radical democracy is a conception of left strategy aimed at unifying a diverse plurality of democratic struggles without privileging the leadership of any specific agent. In the late twentieth century, as the Cold War came to an end and 'actually existing socialism' disintegrated in the face of an ideologically reinvigorated and globalizing capitalism, it was through such a conception that hegemony was fundamentally recast.

Identifying openly as 'Post-Marxists' – implying both a break and continuity – proponents of radical democracy sought to salvage the anti-capitalist critiques and social movement alliances of the socialist and Marxist traditions by dispensing with the 'essentialist' and universalist principles that privileged social classes. More than just a label for the ideological power of the dominant classes, hegemony was transformed into a sophisticated and nuanced category to explain how social identities are contingently recruited to political causes. The Post-Marxist reinvention of hegemony opened up a whole research programme analysing hegemonic contests with numerous types of discourse and identity. It also supported a broad political project that challenged liberal individualism in favour of radically expanding – rather than simply replacing – democracy.

The Post-Marxist approach enabled hegemony to survive the painful defeats of socialism and to enter the twenty-first century as a major concept in contemporary political theory. It put the concept into renewed circulation as a critical theoretical tool for social and political scientists. As a consequence, hegemony remains integral to the dominant paradigms of contemporary critical thought.

Politics in Fragments

What intellectual and political conditions led to the emergence of Post-Marxism? Western Marxists had assumed their analyses of hegemony would contribute to the preparation of a broad alliance for socialism, promoting the interests of the working class as the linchpin for numerous other emancipatory demands. But the success of the Reagan administrations and the Thatcher governments made painfully clear that the right, not the left, had been more adept at generating popular leadership. The growing diversity of social movements and democratic struggles after 1968 had *not* uniformly aligned behind class politics, whether of the 'labourist' or the revolutionary socialist variety.

Thus, the left that had been in the cultural ascendent in the 1960s and 1970s eventually fell into fragments politically and, by the mid-1980s, had been electorally trounced in the US and the UK. There, as we saw, the New Right had gained the initiative, demonstrating that the social democratic management of welfare states no longer commanded automatic or widespread consent. For West European socialists, the USSR had long since lost its status as a beacon – if a flawed one – of anti-capitalism; and new types of radical politics were maturing around, rather than wholesale revolution, discrete struggles for autonomy and recognition, such as 'second-wave' feminism, anti-racism, lesbian and gay politics, or ecologism. Although many of the latter were initially inclined to socialism as a general label for mutual solidarity, collectivism, and equality, they were less enamoured with class politics. The success of the right demonstrated that a reinvigorated individualism, rather than collectivism, could be highly popular. That success was only reinforced with the fall of the Berlin Wall in 1989 and the dissolution of the Soviet Union two years later, which brought the Cold War to an end.

If the shape and purpose of left politics was in doubt, so too was its confidence in an objectively grounded critique of power. Marxism was in crisis as a combined source of critical ideas and a model of universal human emancipation. The very idea of a unifying 'grand narrative' of history, as philosopher Jean-François Lyotard argued in his treatise on the 'post-modern condition', was rapidly losing its force (Lyotard 1984). Indeed, the idea of Enlightenment reason itself – understood as a mode of enquiry that guaranteed the objectivity and accuracy of 'scientific' propositions – was increasingly in question. Critiquing power on that basis was regarded with suspicion, particularly in light of Soviet socialism's authoritarianism and the continued forms of exploitation and domination in the 'free' West.

Much of that doubt was reinforced by the insights of innovative French thinkers, who highlighted how the modern faith in reason obscured its own violent occlusions and complicity in domination. Three are worth briefly noting, since their ideas all contributed in some way to the recasting of hegemony as a project of radical democracy: Michel Foucault, Jacques Lacan, and Jacques Derrida.

Foucault's historical and theoretical analyses rejected the way power was traditionally conceived as something to 'capture' and 'command' so as to impose order. That notion, he argued, was inherited from arguments about sovereignty that privileged the idea of a centralized legal authority (Foucault 1980: 122). Consequently, power was predominantly understood by liberals and Marxists alike as a unified resource for controlling others, and 'freedom' meant escaping its clutches. But, for Foucault, power was not a homogeneous, instrumental force that (like a weapon) functioned only to repress. Rather, it was a 'multiple and mobile field of force relations' (Foucault 1978: 102) that (like language) worked 'strategically' to organize and incite behaviours. Far from a limit on freedom, power positively *produced* subjects through forms of knowledge – such as systems of classification or techniques of bodily control and self-conduct – that named and ordered the world, rendering it amenable to statements of 'truth': for example, knowledge about madness, criminality, sex, or population management (see Foucault 1977). To understand power properly, we needed to trace, 'genealogically', the formation of the 'discourses' – systems of 'power-knowledge' – that, once codified, brought into being organizations such as the state or economy. Beneath the appearance of institutional authority and cohesion (for example, of medicine or education), there were more complex circuits, networks, and 'disciplines' of thinking and acting – discursive 'rationalities' assembled through accounting or information management – that, together, constituted institutions and 'normalized' types of subjectivity.

Similarly, Lacan's psychoanalytic seminars and writings had, since the 1950s, disputed the very idea of a secure, rational subject who could fully know itself and its world (see Lacan 2006). Radicalizing Freud's insights, Lacan viewed the subject as an entity founded on an intrinsic split from its unconscious, or what he called a 'lack'. Rather than possessing an integral identity – built on a stable and independent 'ego' – the Lacanian subject was alienated from the unconscious forces propelling its desires. It was therefore perpetually identifying through images and symbols that promised to satisfy its desires and restore its selfhood (Lacan 2013). 'Imaginary' and 'symbolic' identifications could never overcome lack, however. Instead, they refigured it as prohibitions or unobtainable objects that focused the subject's desires around an unachieved fullness, encouraging it to 'mis-recognize' itself as something that *could* be satisfied and so restored to integrity. However, such 'fantasies' were perpetually vulnerable to failure, threatening individuals with psychic anxiety and so provoking further retreats into fantasy. Lacan was thus deeply sceptical of revolutionary claims to bring about utopian schemes of liberation. Grand ambitions for collective satisfaction were more likely, he suggested, to bring further domination (Lacan 2007: 207).

Finally, Derrida's philosophy of 'deconstruction' criticized what he viewed as the authoritarian underpinnings of reason itself. Language, he argued, was not a transparent medium that captured its object in its 'full presence', without remainder or exclusion. It worked by way of *différance* – that is, through symbolic differences and the temporal deferral of presence, or 'self-identity'. No unchangeable 'centre' provides a linguistic structure (or any other type of structure) with a fixed point of reference that guarantees it stability over time (Derrida 1978: 278–93). Thus, the condition of all communication is that, to work at all, it must be open to repetition, generating a modified meaning in a new context (Derrida 1988). To try to prevent this – by asserting some 'universal' conceptual foundation or appealing to a moral or empirical identity – is to enact a 'metaphysical' violence that refuses the unavoidable impurity (and creativity) of language. Derrida wasn't arguing for intellectual disorder but, rather, for an ethical attentiveness to the damaging conceptual binaries and hierarchies that pervade social and political discourse in the name of universal truth.

Of course, these are all different intellectual enquiries – although now they are associated under the generic label of 'post-structuralism' – and none simply aligns with the other. But they became important reference points for critical thinking in the 1980s and 1990s. They disputed prevailing Marxist assumptions that had underpinned debates about hegemony: that power was concentrated in one locus and utilized by a class agent who imposed it on others; that a collective subject could, once it had recognized its interests, bring liberation to all others; and that the purpose of theoretical enquiry was to find a language that accurately mirrored reality in order to achieve a truly liberated and reconciled society.

As confidence in Marxism receded, the insights of post-structuralists inspired new theoretical approaches and political positions that are broadly defined as Post-Marxist (Sim 2000). The work of Foucault, Lacan, and Derrida (among others) diminished the appeal of 'grand narrative' explanations and 'total' critiques of power. Instead, critics now repudiated 'essentialist' forms of analysis and politics (Gilbert 2008: 49–57). Essentialism is the view that identity hinges on a quality or feature that is complete and unchanging, rather than dependent on the contingent (linguistic, social, historical) relations through which it is formed. Foucault, Lacan, and Derrida all rejected the view that the object of their enquiries could be known outside such relations. All power and identity was partial, open-ended, contextual. These views were particularly well received by critical thinkers traditionally on the margins of Marxist analysis and politics – feminists, and analysts of sexuality and race. As the left struggled politically to combat the New Right, anti-essentialist ideas came to greater prominence. Eventually, the concept of hegemony underwent similar revision.

Deconstructing Marxism

The short volume *Hegemony and Socialist Strategy: Towards a Radical Democratic Politics*, by Ernesto Laclau (1935–2014) and Chantal Mouffe (1943–), was published in 1985. In it, they offered an original account of left politics explicitly characterized as Post-Marxist. Drawing on the work of figures such as Foucault, Lacan, and Derrida, they pressed home the need to conceive radical political strategy as a project of building democratic coalitions from diverse social movements, not as the preparation of a class-based revolutionary transformation. This strategy foregrounded a hegemonic politics, they argued, because it entailed aligning multiple interests and demands behind a common democratic project. But their account of hegemony was not embedded in a theory of capitalist structures or class ideology; it wasn't a formal requirement of the economic 'base' or a situation imposed by the failure of the working class to fulfil its ascribed historic role. For them, hegemony described the political constitution of any social order.

How did Laclau and Mouffe get to this argument? Separately, both had participated in the Marxist debates about hegemony in the 1970s, which sought to reconcile social movement politics to the assumed necessity of class leadership (see Laclau 1977; Mouffe 1979). Laclau was an Argentinian scholar who had experienced Peronist populism as a student activist, and Mouffe, originally from Belgium, taught philosophy at a university in Colombia in the 1960s. Both were, consequently, familiar with Latin America's social movement politics. Hegemony, each argued in their early work, had always hinged on an appeal to a unifying collective identity, independent of class interests. But, then, the 'necessity' of class to hegemony amounted more to an assertion than a logical deduction. Following the analysis by Stuart Hall of Thatcherism and the anti-essentialism of post-structuralist thinkers, Laclau and Mouffe later moved to the view that hegemony had no *necessary* basis in class, declaring: 'It is no longer possible to maintain the conception of subjectivity and classes elaborated by Marxism' (1985: 4). That didn't mean actual classes had no part at all – only that nothing predetermined that class agents or their demands would supply the primary content of hegemonic leadership. To make that point, they set about deconstructing Marxism in order to develop a new theoretical framework.

For Laclau and Mouffe, hegemony needed finally to be decoupled from a Marxist framework. A substantial part of *Hegemony and Socialist Strategy* is therefore devoted to tracing the concept's emergence as a device to mitigate the failure of Marxism's predictions that capitalist societies would polarize into two, opposed classes, with the working class eventually leading its allies to a new, emancipated order. Where the actual structure of society was more complicated, and thus unable to generate the required revolutionary consciousness, hegemony would be invoked 'to fill a hiatus that had opened in the chain of historical necessity' (1985: 7). With Gramsci, however, hegemony was conceived as the principle of social order in general: society did not cohere around a closed economic structure that determined its essential direction. Its unity was only conferred politically – that is, by partial and contingent efforts to forge compromises and minimize conflicts between different social sectors (1985: 65–71). Taking that argument further, Laclau and Mouffe renounced the view that the agents of hegemony had to be economic classes at all (thereby rejecting what they saw as Gramsci's residual 'economism'). Without this foundation in a determining structure, hegemony and its analysis needed a new, more nuanced vocabulary.

How then, according to Laclau and Mouffe, does hegemony work? For them, it names the 'political logic' that gives form to 'the social'. Society, they underline, is not like a material object that imposes physical limits on what can be done. Rather, extending Foucault, it is a 'discursive formation', a complex overlapping series of different social practices best understood through the term 'discourse'. Discourse, they argue, is not purely a 'cognitive' phenomenon, such as ideology or language. It describes a pattern of rule-governed relations, and so can be both material (like a game, where unspoken rules specify the number, place, and behaviour of players) or linguistic (like speech or text). Understood as a set of relations, discourse is intrinsically open-ended, as Derrida had argued: its internal rules can always, in principle, be transformed, thereby modifying the meaning of the elements that make it up. For example, a knife means one thing when it is 'laid' alongside other cutlery on a table, and something quite different when waved around at the counter in the post office. Society, understood as a discursive formation, is intrinsically 'incomplete': 'There is no single underlying principle fixing – and hence constituting – the whole field of differences' (1985: 111). Any order and coherence is a consequence of partially fixing a number of 'nodal points' – key discursive connections – so as to confer form on the whole.

Hegemony for Laclau and Mouffe names the political practice of 'articulating' – or connecting – multiple discourses (such as social customs, institutions, ideas and principles, and forms of knowledge), such that their elements appear as integral moments of a coherent 'totality' ordered around key principles (1985: 113). Thus, Thatcherism had articulated discourses of the nation, law and order, the role of government, ideas of individual freedom, and so on, to a moralistic narrative and a political programme. The contest for hegemony is one in which social groups compete to modify and align these discourses – and the social groups who identify with them – to their own ordering principles, seeking to lead by defining what it is that intrinsically unifies society. In that way, Thatcherism successfully made the free market the central ordering principle, to which could be connected other discourses concerning the role of the state, individual responsibility, and the regeneration of society through entrepreneurial activity.

Importantly, what makes hegemonic discourses cohere is not any internal logic or essence. Indeed, discourses can be highly contradictory. Their coherence, argued Laclau and Mouffe, stems instead from the presence of 'antagonism'. An antagonism is the designation of an external limit on society that blocks its full constitution: 'the presence of the

"Other" prevents me from being totally myself' (1985: 125). An antagonism is more like having an enemy than coming across a contradiction (which denotes a logical impossibility), with all the visceral and affective intensity that conjures. Hegemonic unification, argue Laclau and Mouffe, is the effect of projecting a common antagonism – that is, identifying a global enemy. What unites 'us' is what threatens us and stops us from objectively being who we are. The threat polarizes multiple discourses behind a single symbolic 'frontier' that separates us from 'them' by creating a 'chain of equivalence' between different 'subject positions' (such as workers, women, environmentalists, and so on). Thus, anti-Fascism names an antagonist (Fascism) that joins in opposition to it a variety of different components such as liberals, communists, democracy, personal freedom, and practices of solidarity. Rather than sharing in proximity to a positive entity, Laclau and Mouffe were saying, hegemony is a unity sustained *negatively*. It is the task of a hegemonic strategy to unify allies discursively by projecting an antagonizing force that prevents everyone's full realization, thereby re-aligning them behind its preferred signifiers and discourses.

Laclau and Mouffe's reconstruction of hegemony initially generated bitter reaction, particularly from the Marxist left whose whole theoretical frame they had rather breezily renounced. For re-imagining radical politics without affirming its roots in economic structures, they were accused of 'idealism', 'voluntarism', and of betraying the radical tradition and the hopes associated with it (see Geras 1987; Rustin 1987; Meiksins-Wood 1999; Joseph 2002). Many of these attacks were launched from the very paradigm they sought to critique, and few adequately grasped or explored Laclau and Mouffe's argument. The latter's point, however, was not to dispute that capitalism was a significant context for radical strategy but, rather, simply that it was the *only* context, and that radical politics was thereby bound by ineluctable necessity to centre working-class struggles and demands. The victory of Thatcherism indicated that the identity of the working class was not essentially inclined to be socialist, but could be articulated in all manner of ways: to the right, the centre, or the left. The secret of hegemony, they implied, was how it revealed all social structures and interests to be, in principle, open to creative re-signification. Indeed, it was precisely because of that openness that a new, more pluralistic and democratic politics was possible.

Subjects of Discourse

The theoretical innovations of Laclau and Mouffe opened up a whole new agenda for radical political analysis. Untethering hegemony from Marxism encouraged exploration of different types and modes of hegemonic politics. It no longer concerned exclusively the structure of capitalism, the capitalist state, a dominant ideology, or the class alliances that sustained them. Instead, there are *multiple* hegemonies present in any society – wherever there is subordination to unequal power relations, there are hegemonic contests to justify and sustain them. There are hegemonies of race, of sex and sexuality, and of elites of various kinds in different social and political contexts. These all co-exist and overlap but can be examined, separately and together, by drawing upon the analytical vocabulary Laclau and Mouffe developed – principally, the theory of discourse.

Discourse theory has since emerged as a distinct mode of radical political analysis. Although the term is used by a variety of approaches in social and political theory (such as the work of Habermas on 'discourse ethics') and linguistics (for example in 'Critical Discourse Theory'), Laclau and Mouffe's version supported a highly mobile form of sociopolitical analysis – combining the examination of practical struggles and the discourses employed to mobilize them (see Laclau and Mouffe 1987). In this, it was assisted by having a scholarly base in Laclau's Centre for Ideology and Discourse Analysis at the University of Essex. Sometimes referred to as 'Poststructuralist Discourse Theory' – to acknowledge the distinctive contribution to it of French thought – their account of discourse and hegemony has developed into an internationally successful research programme (Torfing 1999; Townshend 2003). Laclau and his fellow researchers explored methods of discourse analysis (Howarth 2000; Glynos and Howarth 2007), and hegemonic and 'counter-hegemonic' discourses in numerous contexts, such as South African Apartheid (Norval 1998), struggles and conflicts over public policy, disputes over race and sexuality (Smith 1994), debates over Europe and the development of the European Union, or ethno-nationalist conflicts (Howarth, Norval, and Stavrakakis 2000; Howarth and Torfing 2005).

Central to these analyses is the category of the *subject*. Marxist analyses had treated social structures and the class alliances supporting them as the objective components and explanatory ground of hegemony. Subjective experience was assumed to be a more or less complex representation of one's position in class structure. Of course, other systems of domination, such as patriarchy or racism, might complicate this representation (which, as we saw, Marxist structuralists acknowledged). One's ideological disposition – the beliefs and values we take as consonant with our experience – never directly relates to one structure alone but is a 'condensation' of overlapping positions. Nonetheless, despite this complexity, ideology was assumed to align ('in the last instance') to an underlying structural principle.

For Laclau, however, the subject is never fully aligned with its position in a structure: 'the location of the subject is that of dislocation ... far from being a moment in the structure, the subject is the result of the impossibility of constituting the structure as such – that is as a self-sufficient object' (Laclau 1990: 41). Following Lacan, he argues that subjective identity consists in a lack that resists being entirely 'filled' – my identity as a teacher, for example, is dislocated (or blocked) by the low pay that stops me enjoying it or by parental duties that prevent me from giving it my full attention. Thus, I never exhaustively align with my structural role. All social identities are therefore experienced as incomplete, and that is what propels subjects to make further identifications: 'A realistic analysis of socio-political processes must therefore abandon the objectivist prejudice that social forces are something, and start from an examination of what they do not manage to be' (1990: 38). It is the purpose of hegemonic discourses, argues Laclau, to respond to the general experience of dislocation and project it onto a specific antagonist.

The Post-Marxist language of hegemony analysis turns on the permutations of the dislocated subject, rather than institutions or social structures as such. The latter are, of course, wholly relevant because subjects arise and are available for recruitment precisely where specific structures fail fully to structure – particularly during social crises. But the operations of discourse are primarily symbolic, and understanding how they work means tracking identity formation and dissolution. Hegemonic discourses articulate signifying elements, placing them in 'chains of equivalence' that join them to others without wholly erasing their difference. Alternating logics of identity and difference describe the way distinct elements (difference) modify their own meaning as they are lined up together (equivalence) against an antagonizing force (Laclau and Mouffe 1985: 127–34). Hegemonic politics was an ongoing metaphorical contest to articulate and disarticulate subjects symbolically, recruiting them through arguments, narratives, and political ideologies.

In later work, Laclau offered the idea of the 'empty signifier' to clarify hegemonic logic (see Laclau 1996: 36–46). An 'empty signifier' is a privileged term that corresponds not to a discrete object but to a missing dimension of social order itself. It names an enigmatic quality – such as justice, freedom, or peace – that links a whole variety of other discourses and signifying elements, such as legal rights, suffrage, or material equality. The empty signifier works because its very emptiness permits different groups and interests to project their own dislocations onto it as a 'universal' quality that encompasses them. Yet it is also an unfulfilled quality – an absence rather than a presence. Justice, democracy, and so on only mobilize social movements because they aren't fully realized, thereby inciting the desire for completion. Hegemonic politics entails appropriating an empty signifier, 'incarnating' this absence such that it embodies the prospect of a reconciled order. That 'utopian' aspect is key to all struggles for hegemony since it kick-starts the elaboration of chains of equivalence. Importantly, the vehicle for this signifier is not only antagonism but, often, a particular person, group, or demand that is magnified into a figure of potentially universal appeal.

For example, as we noted in the previous chapter, Donald Trump's successful 2016 US presidential campaign was organized around populist signifiers of absent 'national' plenitude 'stolen' by progressive elites, and by his ambition to 'Make America Great Again', encouraging a variety of radical conservative, libertarian, and disaffected social groups and classes to perceive their demands as realizable through his leadership. Alternatively, the murder in the US in 2020 of black man George Floyd, during his arrest by a police officer, sparked protests that triggered a chain of equivalences connecting various citizens and movements around the world, principally via the group Black Lives Matter. Floyd, we might say, came momentarily to incarnate the universal principle of an absent racial justice.

Laclau and Mouffe's model of hegemony stimulated the development of a new generation of critical researchers and political analysts outside the Marxist tradition. In accomplishing this, they salvaged hegemony from its postwar roots in Marxian political sociology and reinvigorated its theoretical foundations. That permitted them to engage productively all sorts of other intellectual traditions – such as psychoanalysis and deconstruction – as well as to explore different types of political conflict. The focus on discourse expanded the scope of hegemony's application but, in part, also domesticated the concept by assimilating it to a general analytics of power. In their attention to discourse, as Forgacs (1989: 88) points out, there was none of Gramsci's 'integral', '"whole-system" view of the social formation'. It was possible, of course, to apply discourse theory to the capitalist state or to political economy (see, for example, Torfing 1998), but that type of encompassing analysis went against the grain of the frequently theoretical and more strategically focused preoccupations of discourse theorists. The retreat to a narrower scale was arguably one consequence of the end of the Cold War and the decline of Marxism as the horizon of radical thinking. Nonetheless, as we shall see in the next chapter, Marxian approaches to international politics and political economy continued to apply hegemony to that wider horizon.

Radical Democracy and Pluralism

As the title of their book indicated, Laclau and Mouffe's re-working of hegemony was originally aimed at transforming socialism into a broader political strategy that conjoined multiple emancipatory demands. Theirs was not a project centred exclusively on overturning capitalism or prioritizing material production over property relations, but, rather, what they called (in their subtitle) a 'radical democratic politics'. For them, socialism – as one project among others seeking freedom from domination – was better understood as a component of a generalized *deepening* of democracy. In that way, Laclau and Mouffe brought back into focus the ethical dimension of hegemony.

The question of democracy had intensified as a point of contention in European socialist movements from the 1970s and 1980s, as social movements contested the automatic primacy of class, and the hierarchical party form, and envisaged the prospect of diverse and participatory forms of democratic struggle (Bloomfield 1977; Hunt 1980). Radical socialists had traditionally criticized parliamentary liberal democracy as an ineffectual, merely 'formal', system that could never return real power to the working class because it would never abolish capitalist property relations. Socialism, by contrast, would substitute parliamentary democracy with a 'substantive democracy' where 'real' control over the means of production was in the hands of the workers. But there was no example where such substantive transformation had actually occurred. Actual socialist states were typically authoritarian regimes that treated their citizens with the deepest suspicion, and governed by radically limiting personal freedom. The Leninist model, in particular, raised serious issues about the compatibility of socialism with democratic freedoms and pluralism. If capitalist democracies were, undoubtedly, limited in the extent to which they challenge property relations, at the very least parliamentary representation permitted *some* degree of accountability, protected freedoms for citizens, and supplied forms of legal redress over civil disputes (Bobbio 1986).

For Laclau and Mouffe, modern socialists should regard themselves as heirs to the 'democratic revolution' that began in the eighteenth century, struggling to deepen and expand democratic protections from domination, rather than replacing it altogether (Laclau and Mouffe 1985: 152–9): 'the alternative of the Left should consist of locating itself fully in the field of the democratic revolution and expanding the chains of equivalence between the different struggles against oppression' (1985: 176). The modern era, they underlined, had led not to the polarization of society around one conflict alone, but to a 'proliferation of antagonisms' across society (1985: 163). So the left ought to foreground a commitment to radical pluralism, rather than promote the interests of one collective subject. Social movements and democratic struggles are inescapably diverse, with different – if occasionally overlapping – objectives. Feminists struggle against patriarchy in its numerous forms; lesbians and gays fight for personal freedom to express their sexuality; ecologists seek measures against industrialization and the ways it damages the environment. There is no reason for these groups automatically or seamlessly to align with each other or with class politics (itself not a singular entity) – they struggle against different types of domination, and experience different kinds of dislocation and antagonism. Thus, the era of the 'radical Jacobin imaginary' – 'the postulation of *one* foundational rupture, and of a *unique* space in which the political is constituted' (1985: 152; italics in the original) – was a romantic ideal that had long passed.

But that doesn't mean parliamentary democracy is all that can be accomplished. Radical democratic pluralism is not liberal individualism; it acknowledges numerous social groups as legitimate subjects and seeks to expand their presence in democratic life. A progressive, non-revolutionary project therefore meant promoting difference, not just equality (1985: 164). The 'democratic imaginary' always entailed combining difference and identity – liberty and equality – and radical democracy had to do likewise, creatively connecting various struggles and demands without homogenizing them, building on the liberal discourse of legal rights but extending them to new social subjects. Radical democracy was thus presented as a way of joining various anti-capitalist and democratic demands without giving automatic priority to overthrowing capitalism as such. For many socialists, of course, that was evidence of apostasy. Laclau and Mouffe, however, argued that anti-capitalism was only one of the left's projects ('there is not *one* politics of the Left') and, in the context of multiple sites of antagonism, socialism could not be the leading principle of a left hegemony.

Against the charge of rehashing political reformism, Mouffe underscored the importance to a radical democratic ethics of the principle of conflict, encapsulated in the concept of 'the political' (see Mouffe 1993, 2000, 2005, 2013). The political, for Mouffe, denotes the domain of contest and antagonism, disagreement and hostility, through which the parameters of any political regime are constituted – as opposed to the domain of 'politics', which concerns the routine exchanges and practices operative within a given, consensually agreed order. With this distinction, Mouffe insists that a left hegemony is distinguished by its appeal to the political – radical democracy can never be envisaged as a harmonious liberal pluralism where antagonism is effectively neutralized in an 'overlapping consensus', as John Rawls put it. Unlike other models of democracy, which seek to found politics on a 'rational' consensus, 'human nature', or some other essential principle, radical democracy promotes 'agonism'. This is a conflictual outlook that refuses the absorption of differences into a bland consensus in the name of a 'fully realized' community. Any political community is the product of hegemony, a precarious outcome of power relations and struggles that is marked by the antagonisms that constitute it:

> a fully inclusive community and a final unity can never be realised since there will permanently be a 'constitutive outside', an exterior to the community that makes its existence possible. Antagonistic forces will never disappear and politics is characterised by conflict and division. Forms of agreement can be reached but they are always partial and provisional since consensus is by necessity based on acts of exclusion. (Mouffe 1993: 69)

Eliminating the dimension of antagonism is to disavow the contingent, political construction of collective interests and so close down the potential to imagine an alternative hegemony. Radical democracy, by contrast, insists on the necessity and inescapability of antagonism – which means that the nature and extent of democratic rights must always be open to 'adversarial' contest (Mouffe 2000: 80–107).

But an 'anti-political' orientation dominates contemporary neo-liberal capitalism, argues Mouffe, by minimizing public disputation in favour of market transactions. Indeed, that was the problem with the UK's post-Thatcher governments of 'New Labour' at the turn of the twenty-first century: they offered a 'politics without adversary' by renouncing conflict for a 'technocratic' model of governance inclined to treat the expansion of markets as a panacea (Mouffe 2000: 108–28). A radical democratic hegemony, she suggested, would not be a toothless 'rainbow' politics but a militant coalition that disputed liberal consensus and argued for the expansion of democratic citizenship.

A Populism of the Left?

In the twenty-first century, both Laclau and Mouffe have defended radical democracy as a type of left-wing 'populism'. As we saw in the last chapter, this describes a project that privileges the antagonism between 'the people' and elites. In the post-Cold War era, and particularly after the global financial crisis of 2008, populist politics of various kinds became increasingly widespread (see Moffitt 2020). For Laclau (whose earliest work was on this topic), populism exemplifies the logic integral to his theory of hegemony: a particular agent comes to articulate a variety of dislocated groups and movements by 'universalizing' itself. All modern politics, he suggests, veers towards an image of the people as an inclusive collective subject struggling against a dominating elite (Laclau 2018). Although populism in the Global North is typically associated with right-wing movements, who limit their notion of the people to an exclusive ethnic group, its underlying logic suggests there is potential for a radical democratic populism. Before his death, Laclau acted as advisor to the centre-left populist Argentinian presidents Néstor Kirchner and Cristina Fernández de Kirchner.

For Mouffe, the recent expansion of populism in Europe is a reaction to the pernicious 'post-political' orientation of recent social democratic governments (Errejón and Mouffe 2016: 22). In trying to govern by narrowing public disagreements and weakening democratic citizenship, antagonism is removed from political cultures. Disaffected and marginalized groups of all kinds (on both the right and the left) are consequently unable to articulate, within existing regimes, the possibility of new forms of collective interest. Therefore, they turn against formal politics and the elites who govern them. Whereas the right tend to specify multiculturalism or immigration as the enemy of social order, a left-wing populism could reasonably be formed around an antagonism towards neo-liberalism, ethno-nationalism, and racism, and in favour of a diverse and inclusive sense of the people. This is particularly so in democracies that have suffered badly from the exclusionary effects of neo-liberal policies during the financial crisis, such as Greece, where traditional social democratic leaders failed to offer substantial opposition in defence of popular concerns. Mouffe herself has contributed to the discussion by the Spanish populist movement Podemos (see Errejón and Mouffe 2016).

Laclau and Mouffe's later attention to populism can be understood as an extension of their earliest interests in Latin American politics, their accounts of radical democracy, and the project to unify numerous social movements. But the success of left-populism has so far been modest. As ever, it remains difficult to sustain a left-wing political movement of disparate parts, and it is not obvious that all components identify sufficiently with the same project. Extending the appeal to 'the people' beyond a coalition of left-wing groups and movements to the wider public remains a substantial challenge (see Prentoulis 2021).

Conclusion

Laclau and Mouffe's recasting of hegemony – by combining a theory of how society is constituted politically with a project of radical democracy – has been the most novel and extensive development of the concept since Gramsci. Building on the Gramscian Marxist legacy, they brought about a paradigm shift in radical political theory. In the context of an increasingly fragmented political landscape in contemporary capitalism and the philosophical criticisms of foundational thought, Laclau and Mouffe reconfigured hegemony in all three of the dimensions highlighted in the introduction.

As a theory of power, they have shifted the accent from a model of state-building focused on classes and institutions to one of collective identity formation focused on discourses. Undoubtedly, that diminishes the presence of sociological concepts – such as the class, state, civil society, intellectuals, or parties – in favour of more abstract coordinates. As they said, 'it is no longer a case of *foundations* of the social order, but of *social logics*' (1985: 183; italics in the original). Yet that attention to logics grants leeway to conceive hegemony as a general model and to apply it to a multiplicity of new and different contexts.

As regards subjectivity, their discourse theory elaborated a complex, anti-essentialist approach to social identity that foregrounds the subject as the primary medium of hegemonic contests. Inevitably, that means institutions and technological mechanisms of identity construction (such as the media) are diminished in favour of general attention to the symbolic content and transformations of identity, though it does not rule out more contextual analysis (see, for example, Dahlberg and Siapera 2007; Dahlberg and Phelan 2011).

Finally, radical democracy reignited the issue of the ethical dimension of hegemony, posing the question of what emancipation could be in a post-industrial, post-socialist age suspicious of certain types of essentialism and universalism (see Butler, Laclau, and Žizek 2000). With its emphasis on pluralism and antagonism, rather than a collective subject seeking societal harmony, radical democracy returned to a realist ethic that accepts emancipation as necessarily partial and incomplete. Nonetheless, that incompleteness is the precondition for radically renewing democratic politics.

5
Beyond the State: Hegemony in the World

Up till now, the frame through which we have explored hegemony's evolution has been largely that of the nation state. This mirrors the preoccupations of Gramsci and those who sought to apply his ideas to postwar politics. But the concept has a longer lineage. In its earliest references, hegemony described how ancient city states would lead multi-state alliances and dominate for periods of time beyond their own borders (Lebow and Kelly 2001). The 'field' over which hegemonic leadership was exercised was initially that of 'external' states, rather than 'internal' communities. In the twentieth century, that leadership function was attributed to the US, whose global dominance has been central to debates about hegemony among the various 'schools' of the discipline of International Relations (IR) (see Ferguson 2005; Worth 2015; Schmidt 2018). For many IR theorists and commentators, what distinguishes politics on an international scale is the absence of the unitary legal or institutional arrangements that define national politics. The proper characterization of international politics is therefore 'anarchy' – there simply is no formal authority or common moral framework governing what *all* states across the world must or must not do. With that condition, the stakes are peculiarly high as 'world order' is perpetually threatened by rivalries and disagreements (see Ashley 1988; Bull 2002).

How does hegemony apply in this wider frame? Because of the assumption of international anarchy, the distinction between coercion/consent, domination/hegemony, is less easily drawn than at a national scale. Order is often associated with the 'supremacy' of one powerful state, or 'hegemon' (or more), either in a particular region or across the globe. But the general status of a hegemonic order remains ambivalent: frequently it is equated *either* with domination by one powerful state over others, *or* with the achievement of consensual leadership among a broad inter-state coalition. The first is the view of conservative proponents of US power in the world who regard hegemonic domination as necessary for world order, but also of left-wing critics, such as Noam Chomsky (2003), who juxtaposes such domination to 'democracy and freedom'. The second is the view of scholars, such as Ian Clark (2011), who, by contrast, regard hegemony as the basis for an 'international society' of shared legitimating norms and institutions.

Is hegemony the enemy or the saviour of world order? Disagreement on this question reflects not only opposed schools of thought but also the inherent ambiguity of hegemony's combination of domination and leadership, albeit magnified in a context where the two are sometimes so intertwined as to be almost indistinguishable. War, conquest, or diplomatic isolation are frequently integral to maintaining consensual alliances and support for international institutions and norms. In international thinking, then, there is considerable contest over what hegemony means and, indeed, what it is that is hegemonic. The international frame of hegemony can be adjusted in various, radically different ways. As we shall see below, in some accounts hegemony concerns principally powerful states and their dominance; for others, it concerns consensual leadership across a system of states through values and institutions; and for recent neo-Gramscian critical theorists, it describes the expansion of an economic order through the combination of force and consent.

Leading the World

In an international context of unequal powers, hostile and aggressive social forces, and fierce competition over territorial boundaries and economic resources, what stops general disorder or even lawlessness breaking out? In the situation of international anarchy, power is revealed as a basic matter of territorial security and political integrity. These are usually not subtle matters of civil co-existence among a settled citizenry occupying a common space, but concern how any common space can be sustained such that it can be ruled at all. For scholars of IR, a persuasive response to the question of order is the argument that states are essentially unitary, self-interested actors whose 'external' behaviour involves a calculation of what lies in their best interests. The choice between war and conquest or peace and cooperation is one that depends on the ongoing assessment of resources and opportunities. In a situation of anarchy, international politics has traditionally followed the Machiavellian logic of rival states calculating how to act in their own advantage.

This perspective on international politics is known as 'realism' or 'neo-realism' (see Morgenthau 1948; Waltz 1979). It assumes that the international field is characterized, in essence, by states that are integral (rather than divided) actors seeking to maximize their advantage (rather than share ideals) in the face of competition with rivals. What determines the behaviour of such states is ultimately their rational assessment of the relative strength of other states and the prospects for their own territorial security and integrity. The international domain is thus a relatively unstructured space in which each state's actions potentially alter the actions of the others. Given such a precarious scenario, only the presence on the world stage of one or more substantially powerful states – in the possession of significant military and/ or financial resources – can diminish the threat of perpetual instability. By holding the 'balance of power', and so guaranteeing that transgressions will be punished, the hegemonic state dominates the wider 'international system' and, in so doing, serves its own interests as others depend on it for their long-term survival (Morgenthau 1948: 125–33). Against what is sometimes thought to be unrealistic faith in shared humanitarian concerns or moral ideals, realists argue that rivalry between states is the basic condition of international politics.

Whatever consensual 'order' there is in the traditional realist view of the world is achieved largely 'passively' by the mere threat of overwhelming force from the hegemon. Yet, if traditional realists equated hegemony with domination, other variants have underscored the likelihood that dominance also enables a deeper, consensual leadership over other states (Keohane 1984). Sometimes referred to as 'hegemonic stability theory', this view highlights how various, structured hierarchical (rather than purely anarchical) orders (or 'regimes') produce sustained inter-state cooperation by way of common rules, principles, and institutions that are underwritten by the power of one or more dominant states. A stable and 'free' world order, from this perspective, is one where states exercise rational self-interest by sharing collective norms and respecting boundaries in light of the possible withdrawal of support by the dominant power. Having a hegemon, then, is in the interests of the weaker states that benefit from it, especially their economic interests. Without such a threat, there would not be, for example, 'economic openness' but narrow self-interest and disorder, although the actual use of force (particularly once an institutional regime is established) is rarely required (Keohane 1984: 184; Webb and Krasner 1989).

Hegemony, then, is sometimes described by realists in terms of 'polarities' where the presence of dominant states helps to define the character of the whole system. For example, international systems may be 'unipolar' (dominance by a single state – the traditional realist view), 'bipolar' (two competing states), or 'multipolar' formations (numerous bases of power). A unipolar system is represented by the global dominance of the British Empire in the nineteenth century (the so-called Pax Britannica); the bipolar system resembles the model of superpower rivalry of the US and the Soviet Union during the Cold War in the twentieth century; and the multipolar system refers, perhaps, to international politics in the current, post-Cold War world (though there is disagreement as to whether the US is now a new, unipolar hegemon). Each configuration describes a distinct, if broad and fluctuating, system of interactions through which various alliances, rivalries, and conflicts are managed. In this last stage, however, hegemony is increasingly weakened as no single centre of power is strong enough to dominate and competitive rivalries increase (among, for example, the US, the Russian Federation, China, and the European Union).

In many ways, the realist outlook – which has been central to IR thinking since the discipline's birth – is the basis for all subsequent approaches to international politics, which usually take issue with some or all of its basic tenets. The meaning of hegemony for realists owes much to a certain reading of Machiavelli that emphasizes states as self-interested agents, and politics as a perpetual competition for advantage, underpinned by violence rather than a set of unifying ideals. If there is, undoubtedly, a sense of the precariousness of power and the centrality of strategic manoeuvres, there is also a strong tendency to think in Hobbesian terms by fixating on 'sovereign' states as the sole possessors of power. Hegemony, for realists, describes something that states seek by virtue of their superior command of resources (although dominance may set in train forms of cooperation and leadership that serve mutual ends). But hegemony never really alters the basic character of these states.

Alternative, less state-centric accounts of international hegemony have, by contrast, given more attention to the character of consensual leadership than to the menacing power of a hegemon. Clark (2011), for example, underlines the importance of hegemony as a form of 'legitimacy'. That is, hegemony describes a complex of shared norms and values among a 'society' of interdependent states, not the attribution of 'primacy' to any individual state. Developing the work of Hedley Bull (2002) and the 'English School' of International Relations theory, Clark regards hegemonic leadership not as an 'optional extra' to domination, consisting of shared ideology and interests with the dominant state but, rather, as *an institutionalised practice of special rights and responsibilities conferred on a state with the resources to lead* (Clark 2009: 24; italics in the original). 'Institutions' are here not merely organizations, but common practices and norms around, for example, war, diplomacy, trade, and so on, through which states observe common responsibilities. Leadership is a status of recognition willingly *granted* to one or more powerful states by others, not a linear extension of economic or military power.

Reversing the direction this way, Clark substitutes realism's narrow focus on the objective dimension of hegemony with attention to a more expansive subjective dimension. This complicates the rigidly simplistic idea of international hegemony as a fixed structure premised on the power of one state by offering a more relational and historically variable account (see Watson 2007). Clark points to the 'dynamics' of legitimacy as a condition of 'voluntary compliance' by states that is highly variable in form and scope. Sometimes this hegemony is 'collective', such as the Concert of Europe in the nineteenth century – the post-Napoleonic legal 'consensus' among the Great Powers and smaller states to respect territorial boundaries and to resolve disputes diplomatically. At other times, hegemony might be 'singular', as with the Pax Britannica which was limited to recognition of Britain's preeminent economic role beyond Europe. The US-led hegemony of the twentieth century, on the other hand, is described by Clark as 'coalitional' since consent for it came from a restricted group of allies who participated in institutions on matters of finance, security, and politics.

For mainstream IR, then, hegemony concerns how international order is structured through hierarchical relations of power among states. For realists, a dominant state is the primary locus of political power, whose foreign policy is vital for the whole system. But, for Clark, politics dissipates across a less hierarchical system of states governed by consensual norms.

Gramsci and International Relations

In mainstream International Relations discourse, hegemony is typically associated with the activities of sovereign states, inter-state organizations and institutions, their elites, and the combination of threats and agreements through which these interact. Marxist approaches to IR, however, place critical focus not exclusively on states and their elites but on the broader capitalist structures and class agents that influence them (see Rosenberg 1994; Joseph 2002). Capitalism has always been understood by Marxists as a globalizing force that ruthlessly obliterates territorial boundaries and other such obstacles in order to exploit opportunities to generate profits. In this, it perpetually challenges claims to institutional authority and independence. How does this change our understanding of hegemony on an international horizon?

There are, of course, significant differences among Marxists as to how to conceive capitalism as a global phenomenon. Lenin, for example, saw 'monopoly capitalism' as a distinct phase in which nation states and financial sectors of capital combined to expand national markets aggressively (Lenin 2010). An 'imperialistic' struggle to find and control new markets was regarded by many Marxists to have led to the First World War. But that theory presents states as mere ciphers of pre-given interests, and is poor at explaining the wide variations and resistances to a competitive logic. Alternatively, 'world systems theory', developed by Immanuel Wallerstein (2004), offers a more complex picture. For Wallerstein, the whole world is a dynamically integrated economic system whose uneven distribution of capital and labour means particular locations operate differently. Not all states bear the same pressures or capacities, yet they must integrate themselves into a world economy in ways that suit their positions among the 'core', 'semi-peripheral', or 'peripheral' locations of the global division of labour. World systems theory replaces monopoly capitalism's emphasis on classes with a more structurally oriented account – national states are interdependent agents of the unequally distributed demands of capital, rather than instruments of dominant classes. In different phases, a hegemonic state emerges to lead other states in the process of sustaining and expanding the world system.

Both these approaches treat states largely as instruments of another source of power – capitalist classes or the uneven structural imperatives of the capitalist system. As a consequence, hegemony (when mentioned at all) tends to be uni-directional, a form of domination that offers little room for politics and strategic compromises beyond the narrow pursuit of class interests. However, an alternative to the realist hypostatization of states, and to the Marxist tendency to diminish them, was initiated by Robert W. Cox in the

1980s (see Cox 1987, 1993). Cox sought to apply Gramsci's insights on hegemony to the field of IR. In this, he underlined the complex and layered interaction of capitalism and states in generating world order.

For Cox, the international supremacy of a state has to be understood in relation to its leading role in expanding a particular model of capitalism. Hegemony should not therefore be conceived as an arbitrary force, or just a 'euphemism for imperialism' (1993: 60). 'World orders', insists Cox, 'are grounded in social relations' (1993: 64). At an international level, hegemony describes historical phases and discrete patterns of 'order within a world economy with a dominant mode of production which penetrates into all countries and links other subordinate modes of production' (1993: 62). A world economy depends on agreeing shared priorities, institutions, and norms that subordinate states will recognize and uphold. Although Gramsci never developed a theory of International Relations, Cox argued that his conceptual architecture is nonetheless highly pertinent to it (see also Morton 2003a; Bieler et al. 2015). Gramsci's conception of the state, especially, highlighted the importance of gradually extending consensual relationships beyond narrow political alliances – and that applies internationally as much as it does domestically: 'The hegemonic concept of world order is founded not only upon the regulation of inter-state conflict but also upon a globally-conceived civil society' (1993: 61).

Accordingly, different phases of international hegemony are underpinned by the expansion of a dominant class's influence beyond its original state borders into a global civil society of international institutions, public and private agencies, organizations, and elites. For example, Cox underscores how the Pax Britannica was premised on the general acceptance of free trade, supported by the gold standard, and recognition of British sea power as a final, coercive guarantor. British hegemony thus secured the conditions for free trade capitalism. Later, following a period of disorder, hegemony was reconstructed on the basis of postwar US leadership (again, the Pax Americana), underpinned by its military dominance, which supported an economic order based on competing trade blocs. In the western sphere, these comprised welfare states with mixed economies and strategies of Keynesian demand management and planning, supported by institutions such as the World Bank and NATO.

Importantly, for Cox, hegemonic world orders are not structurally given by the distribution of material power alone, but are political and ideological achievements. Drawing upon Gramsci's concepts of 'war of position' and 'historic bloc', he presents hegemony as the consequence, first, of struggles and compromises among 'social forces' (classes, but also other social groups and elites) at a national level to achieve domestic hegemony around a dominant system of production. Then, once hegemony is secured at a national level, it is possible to expand beyond state boundaries to facilitate – by way of principles, values, norms, and rules of conduct accepted as 'universally' applicable – the broader, international environment, extending to peripheral states and neutralizing resistance: 'A world hegemony is thus in its beginnings an outward expansion of the internal (national) hegemony established by a dominant social class. The economic and social institutions, the culture, the technology associated with this national hegemony become patterns for emulation abroad' (1993: 61).

Of course, this expansion is a long, slow process of building institutions and making compromises that, more than simply securing one state's advantage, embed a stable configuration of relations that conjoin structured interests, political organizations, and ideological principles. Inter-state arrangements on trade, for example, help to align policy objectives and coordinate policies, diminish conflicts, and cultivate elites with similar skills and ideological outlooks – all of which ensures the 'dominant state takes care to secure the acquiescence of other states according to a hierarchy of powers within the inter-state structure of hegemony' (1993: 63).

Cox's alternative to realism laid the basis for a strain of 'neo-Gramscian' analyses, particularly in International Political Economy (see Gill 1993; Morton 2003b; Worth 2015: 71–6). It stimulated research with a distinctly historical focus on the variations and changes in international capitalism, particularly regarding the global leadership of the

US (see, for example, Augelli and Murphy 1988; Gill 1990; Rupert 1995). In this, a refreshing awareness of political struggles over power was returned to the discussion of international hegemony. Like Clark (discussed above), Cox understood hegemony as a model of consensual leadership among states, not the dominance of a coercive force alone. Unlike Clark, however, he insisted on connecting consent to deeper economic processes and social forces, seeing these as part of a worldwide effort to lead the expansion of particular productive interests. As Worth points out, however, his state-centric focus on periods of world order nonetheless brought him to similar conclusions to hegemonic stability theory (Worth 2015: 70–1).

Indeed, Cox's extension of Gramscian concepts to the international field garnered criticism from a number of quarters (see Burnham 1991; Germain and Kenny 1998; Femia 2005). It was noted, for example, that whereas Gramsci understood civil society to be organically linked to the nation state, a 'global civil society' is not the same kind of domain. A national civil society is a set of more or less bounded associations integrated through 'national-popular' projects. A global civil society, on the other hand, is much more diffuse and unevenly integrated, pragmatically oriented, and not overtly aligned to any single state or to a uniform class project. It is therefore less amenable to the nationally focused consensus building initiatives that Gramsci had suggested.

Applying Gramsci's ideas internationally, in Worth's assessment, remains 'confused' if hegemony is modelled only on the spatial expansion of a single power (2015: 76). But if we shift focus from dominant states to the ideological and institutional strategies through which they pursue a certain order, we might gain a more nuanced understanding of how new capitalist priorities are consolidated. That way, hegemony can describe a much more uneven *process* of establishing a dominant economic order than an exclusively state-led project (see Robinson 2005). As Worth suggests, in this respect 'hegemony should be viewed through the lens of an overriding ideology, rather than through the lens of a state' (2015: 107). This point is particularly pertinent to the analysis of an emergent, global world order.

A New Global Order?

For a while, globalization became the buzzword of popular and academic debate, particularly after the collapse of Soviet and East European communism, which brought an end to the Cold War but also to the realistic prospect of an alternative to capitalism. Excitement grew in the 1990s over national barriers breaking down and old conflicts becoming obsolete, giving way to a new, more globally integrated world. Globalization described the expansion of trade, the growth of markets, and new opportunities for employment and consumption (Hirst and Thompson 1999). It also involved the proliferation of technologies, which fostered an increasingly 'connected' world through communicative 'networks' unhindered by territorial boundaries (Castells 2010). The era of the nation state was in apparent retreat and a more open, but also uncertain, world beckoned (Holton 1998). What kind of world order would that be?

As globalization progressed, mainstream IR scholars debated what role the US should have in this new environment. Was it now a unipolar hegemon or, in a multipolar world, simply 'in decline'? How would its dominance even be measured, given that the threat of the Soviet Union had disappeared (Worth 2015: 60–1)? Various examples of US-led military interventions (for example, in Iraq and Afghanistan) may give the impression that unipolar domination was the role being sought. The Islamist attacks on the US in September 2001 certainly provoked a break with the relative optimism of the early post-Cold War era, bringing 'hawkish' realist principles back to the surface. But, on the whole, such interventions have been selective and are, in any case, unsustainable over the long term. Still, even for less conservative thinkers, the US emerged from the Cold War with a 'crisis of authority' that needed to be resolved. Rather than assert its coercive power, however, it is argued by some that the US needs to re-establish its authority as the leader of an international order of strong liberal institutions (Ferguson 2005; Ikenbury 2011). Alternatively, Clark (2009) suggests that there is a role for the US in implanting a new form of international society over the long term. The US certainly remains the leading global power, and hence the only one available for that task, but any new international order requires it to enhance organizations such as the United Nations, among others, where liberal rules and freedoms are collectively established.

For neo-Gramscians, by contrast, the new global order is less about reconstituting the authority of the US and more about expanding a world productive order. That order is premised on the extension of market economic principles to almost every area of life, thereby disrupting settled boundaries and generating new hostilities. As a general process, globalization is associated by Marxists and radical critics with 'neo-liberalism' – that is, the aggressive promotion of market mechanisms throughout the world. Far from a benign form of liberal order, neo-liberalism is often an invasive, disciplinary force that operates largely unchecked by any kind of national democratic politics (Harvey 2005). Though often described as a 'natural' or rational extension of market principles (Gray 2009), in fact globalization constitutes a deliberate political and ideological project. It involves institutionalizing economic power through the expanded application of market mechanisms and the opening of domestic economies to international competition and investment, de-industrialization of the productive core and relocation of production to newly industrialized countries, deregulation, privatization, intensified reliance on new technologies, and a relinquishing of the welfare role of states in favour of market discipline to increase competitiveness (Rupert 2000). Embedding these conditions (which vary from state to state) demands significant domestic adjustments to policy by nation states, and the forging of new alliances and hierarchies.

For Gill and Law (1993), this global order instantiates a movement towards a new 'historic bloc' – that is, a distinct articulation of material economic forces and forms of ideological and political organization – led by a so-called 'transnational' class of financiers and corporations less inclined to seek out compromises with states. Global capitalism thus entails a radical shift in the power of transnational capital over national capital (1993: 105–13). Where 'Fordist' strategies had integrated economics and politics by incorporating workers into democratic states through welfare arrangements, global capitalism now seeks to *separate* economic from political arrangements. Nation states and international organizations must accommodate transnational corporations: keep wages low, decrease the burden of taxation, supply skilled workers, and enable savings through technological innovation, and so on. Meanwhile, organized labour is perpetually struggling against the threat of unemployment, the weakening of trade union rights, and the loss of benefits (such as pensions) gained under former hegemonic settlements.

Transnational corporations have achieved an influence in institutions of global governance, such as intergovernmental bodies like the OECD and institutions such as the IMF, the World Trade Organization, the World Bank, or the Trilateral Commission. Networks of financial interests service elite connections and reinforce shared strategic goals supporting the global mobility of capital (Gill and Law 1993: 102–4). These networks are enforced in inter-state agreements such as the so-called 'Washington Consensus', which links indebted states to a requirement to restructure their economies in line with stringent market-based principles (Worth 2015: 95–8). Gill and Cutler argue that national institutions are being shaped by a 'new constitutionalism' – the promotion of legal, political and ethical arrangements to embed what is described as 'disciplinary neo-liberalism' (Gill and Cutler 2015). This refers to a project of 'market civilization' based on a bloc of forces supporting highly globalized capital. Although unevenly implemented, constitutionalism aims to institutionalize legal and political arrangements that enable competition, enhance market opportunities, and delegitimize the prospect of forms of solidarity shaping political orders.

But it would be mistaken here to assume that hegemony describes some fixed and inescapable structure of domination. On the contrary, other neo-Gramscian analyses underline the open-ended character of the global 'power bloc' (Rupert 2000: 15). Rather than a solid structure of power, neo-liberalism is a disruptive process of innovation and transformation that 'fixes' only temporarily onto particular scales and sites of productive activity – such as cities which have a unique density of populations and capital (Brenner 2004) – and these do not always align effectively with other national or international spatial scales or sites (Jessop 2002). Rather than being homogeneous units, individual states are compelled selectively to adjust their own national and international strategies, prioritizing certain locations over others, as opportunities arise to enhance competition and trajectories of economic growth. Neo-liberal strategies may require coordination and negotiation across states but, as a consequence, the kind of hegemony they achieve is unlikely to be the type of stable, long-term settlement achieved in the West in the decades after the war.

Global Subjects

With this changing articulation of production and governance have come new modes of consent. These typically make appeals to the 'sovereign consumer', understood as the privileged subject of a globalizing world. In highlighting the consensual basis of hegemony, mainstream IR approaches dwell on inter-state political agreements or normative frameworks of legitimacy. As critics, however, neo-Gramscians underline the contradictory, and popularly contested, dimensions to any neo-liberal consensus (Rupert 2000). Admittedly, they have tended to stick to a familiar Marxist focus on class ideologies (broadly, expressions of interests), rather than employ the more expansive notions of culture and discourse referenced by Post-Marxists (see Worth 2015: 76–85). Nonetheless, they contribute to a wider radical critique of neo-liberalism as ideologically driven strategies that involve the installation of new ways of experiencing and rationalizing personal and collective identity.

For example, one of the compelling features of much 'global discourse' has been the embrace of 'universal' values connected to a benign, diverse, and inclusive world. In contrast to an earlier world order built around the defence of national traditions and loyalties to particular cultures, global changes are argued to 'dis-embed' self-identity and encourage a subjective 'reflexivity' that expands our sense of responsibility beyond a single place (see Giddens 1991). Indeed, ideas of social identity are increasingly conceived as multifaceted, and pliable, and endorsed as part of a world looking beyond narrow borders, hierarchies, and ingrained customs. However, critics highlight how such ideas mirror and service the logic of global capital. Neo-liberal economies encourage consuming citizens to interact, purchase, and invest as subjects in a world of limitless opportunity. What holds us back is not the world itself, only our own lack of preparation as 'entrepreneurs'. Thus, we are compelled perpetually to invest in ourselves, to re-educate ceaselessly, so that we can 'flexibly' adapt and make ourselves 'resilient' to the challenges of the new global economy (Chandler and Reid 2016). This, say its critics, is a perverse ideology that obscures profound structural inequalities around the world and, by isolating individuals under the guise of 'empowerment' and 'choice', degrades human autonomy in order to exploit any possible source of value for profit.

Once, globalization was viewed by liberals as an opportunity for greater dialogue in new forms of devolved and 'cosmopolitan' democracy (see Held 1995; Archibugi 2008). But the experience has often been much less progressive or liberating. The sovereign consumer is not the self-aware, civic-minded, and autonomous liberal subject who acts rationally in concert with others, but, rather, an insecure subject who has constantly to bear risks and suffer the perpetual indignities of market self-discipline in an unpredictable world economy that constantly narrows the horizon of emancipation. Democracy has often been 'hollowed out' and undermined as collective choices are off-loaded to agencies at a distance from actual publics. Global transformations, neo-Gramscians remind us, offer what Gramsci called a 'passive revolution' – radical structural change but without the active mobilization of popular consent (Morton 2007). This is frequently the experience of international hegemony on the capitalist periphery, where economic modernization and liberalization have often come about by way of military dictatorships (see Munck 2013; Hesketh 2019). Neo-liberal world 'order' in general has turned out to be somewhat uneven, unstable, and, for many, insecure. In addition to huge and growing disparities in wealth and employment opportunities, new wars and global conflicts – such as the interventions after September 2001 or the devastations of the civil war in Syria – have generated poverty, migration, and refugee crises that call into question the capacity for nation states to cooperate effectively at a higher level.

Instead of greater democratic inclusion and consent, market ideology (and the geopolitical manoeuvres undertaken to extend it) has provoked increased reaction and hostility. The rise of 'fundamentalist' politics – notably, Islamist terrorism – and the growth of overt hostility to immigration in western democratic states suggests a narrowing, not a broadening, of social and political identities. Conservative reaction and resentment in the form of radical right-wing populism (noted in chapter 3) has been a salient development in global politics, signalling the limits to popular consent. Indeed, angry and abusive online cultures have proliferated, disrupting and displacing mainstream national media with cynical 'culture wars' or puritanical campaigns against establishment mores (see Nagle 2017). The election of President Trump and the success of Brexit in the UK, for example, suggest that neo-liberalism is capable of provoking significant resistance in its own heartlands. Despair at inequality and insecurity (and anger at the elites who defended them over decades) has resulted in deeply resentful subjects, many of whom look to assertions of religious or racial 'community' to protect them from neo-liberal hegemony, even if these mean undemocratic or even violent types of action.

Such developments underline that the positive story neo-liberal elites and states promote has never fully achieved hegemonic status, if by that we mean *total* domination of the minds and attitudes of ordinary people. Rather, neo-liberal hegemony is better understood as an uneven project that meets popular resistance, even as it succeeds in winning over elites and nation states.

Counter-Hegemony

Unlike mainstream IR writers on hegemony, who are largely in favour of it and regard a US-led world as the source of a stable, pragmatic, and open international system, neo-Gramscians are largely opposed. As Marxists (and in keeping with anti-capitalists generally), they regard neo-liberal hegemony as a pernicious and unjust project that limits human freedom and subordinates vast swathes of the world to a relentless logic of exploitation. As noted above, they are wary that elite institutions and transnational alliances effectively by-pass democracy, enforcing passive revolutions in national social and political architectures. For these reasons, they often support popular radical, indigenous, and anti-capitalist social movements and class struggles to emancipate people from the power of transnational corporations and neo-liberal governance.

This critical stance is frequently described as support for a 'counter-hegemony'. Now, Gramsci did not use the term 'counter-hegemony' – his aim was not to 'counter' capitalism but to replace it by building a new hegemonic order. That aspiration, however, is unlikely in a global era where no alternative international 'historic bloc' is available (as Gramsci believed there was in the 1930s via the Soviet Union). As Cox put it: 'one tactic for bringing about change in the world order can be ruled out as a total illusion. There is very little likelihood of a war of movement at the international level through which radicals would seize control of the superstructure of international institutions' (1993: 64). Instead, he continued: 'We must shift the problem of changing world order back from international institutions to national societies.' Counter-hegemony often implies holding back and refusing the tide of capitalist expansion by supporting local struggles and building alliances from the subaltern classes at the 'base' who advocate for an alternative bloc (Morton 2007: 171–200).

This general orientation supports an emancipatory ethic based on numerous demands for 'social justice', particularly among the powerless, the indigenous, and the disadvantaged across the Global North and South. Such demands are exemplified in, for example, the 'Occupy' movement in the US, the 'Zapatista' communities in Mexico (see Morton 2007: 190–7), as well as events such as the European Social Forum and other efforts to generate dialogue around alternatives to neo-liberal globalization. These are typically highly diverse movements with different methods and distinct stakes in their forms of resistance. But often they are uniquely international in outlook, explicitly connecting local, national, or regional forms of opposition to expanding structures of global domination. A counter-hegemonic movement is therefore unlikely to take the form of Gramsci's revolutionary Modern Prince. But, for some, it remains plausible to imagine a diverse network, or 'collective intellectual', of popular movements across civil society emerging to unify and coordinate these struggles (Morton 2007: 207–8).

In key respects, this brings some neo-Gramscian positions on counter-hegemony into line with Post-Marxists who advocate for radical democracy, and who also see themselves as opponents of neo-liberalism. Mouffe, for example, argues for a 'multipolar' world order and a 'democratic transnationalism' that incorporates civil society movements and popular assemblies (Mouffe 2005: 90–118). Against liberal proponents of 'cosmopolitan democracy', which Mouffe thinks erases the diversity and unevenness of international space, she proposes a new equilibrium of regional world blocs to promote pluralism and the recognition of difference. Moreover, Laclau and Mouffe's appeal to left-populism converges with the notion of a diverse and contingent 'movement of movements' to rally subaltern and anti-capitalist groups.

Conclusion

Exploring hegemony at an international level draws our attention to the wider horizon of politics beyond the borders of nation states, which, simultaneously, influences how states themselves function. Nation states are deeply bound up with the strategic foreign and trade policy choices and structural economic processes unfolding across the world, and that is ever more so in an age of globalizing capitalism. But in surveying references to hegemony in international politics, it is clear the term is given contrasting meanings and functions, particular to specific schools of thought. For some, it means the preponderance of one powerful state in a wider system; for others, it highlights the shared norms and institutions that bind a system of states to a certain world order. Yet others view it as the uneven expansion of a system of material production. Each account has a different focus on power, and a different sense of how force and consent combine. Moreover, each points to a different view of the ethical implications of hegemony, with conservative, liberal, and radical approaches all having their own, incompatible, perspectives. It is clear that, at this level, employing hegemony is more complicated than it is within a nation state. The major difference from 'domestic' accounts of hegemony is the absence of more or less settled boundaries and a single, permanent authority that unifies political space. International hegemony is therefore burdened to explain a range of phenomena that no one theoretical approach can easily hold within its scope. Doubtless, international politics is characterized simultaneously by powerful states seeking to assert regional or global authority, by institutional regimes that share norms and hold other states to account, and by material interests and processes setting and subverting limits to economic interaction. And wherever hegemony is identified, it is always possible to find it being contested. However it is employed, it is perhaps better to think of international hegemony as a means to alert us to processes rather than to a solid structure; to a direction of travel, with many actual and possible diversions, rather than to an exclusive or final destination. This is particularly so in the case of neo-liberal globalization, which, at any moment, is associated with the domination of one state or several states, with transnational classes and their influence in international institutions, with disciplinary ideologies and modes of subjectivity, but also with forms of resistance that expose limits or hold back the tide of international forces.

International approaches also serve, therefore, to underscore hegemony's status as an interpretive frame with choices to be made about how to apply it. As we'll see in the next chapter, however, these choices – with their focus principally on forms of leadership aiming to assert some direction on various other forces – may also be regarded as restrictive, rather than illuminating. Is there, we might ask, a politics without hegemony?

6
The End of Hegemony?

The success of hegemony in the twentieth century lay in its ability to pose questions about the nature of power and domination. In treating power as a malleable field of relations rather than a fixed or imposed order, hegemony presents politics (or the struggle for power) as a strategic activity of incrementally extending leadership, transforming actual or potential opponents into supporters, and so on. Structures of domination – such as the state, economic, or cultural systems – are not closed, self-sustaining regimes, but social constructions that, with coordinated direction, can be rendered morally or intellectually acceptable. The focus and scope of hegemony alter in different approaches, as we have seen, but its analytical strength derives from this central insight. From it then emerge questions concerning hegemony's basic dimensions: what particular strategies and alliances sustain power? How are subjects persuaded to endorse it? What alternative relations to power can be wrested from it?

However, if hegemony displaces power and domination from a single locus onto a broader (strategically organized) field, nonetheless does it not continue to replicate the idea of there being a unifying centre? Is not hegemony merely a *fictive* substitute for a disavowed reality, rather than a rejection of it altogether? The uncertain line separating leadership and domination suggests that power can never be eradicated, only negotiated differently. As a consequence, some critics are suspicious that, if taken to be thematic of politics in general, the concept reproduces the very thing it purportedly opposes: a statist politics that prioritizes unity over diversity, or identity over difference. 'Counter-hegemony' may appear to destabilize structures of domination, but it remains implicitly attached to the same type of ordering principle. Far from acknowledging the inescapable complexity of the world and liberating differences, it is argued, hegemony only returns us to a stultifying politics of mastery. If radical political critique is genuinely to promote justice and emancipation, then hegemony needs to be brought to an end. As some argue, contemporary modes of power and resistance should be characterized as 'post-hegemony' (Lash 2007; Beasley-Murray 2010).

In this final chapter, I explore critical responses to hegemony as a general framework for understanding power and politics. More than just critiques of its empirical scope or focus, these regard hegemony as a defunct mode of analysis – a somewhat clunky concept from a state-centric era that is unreceptive to the way contemporary power operates and, therefore, unable to offer genuinely creative ways to resist it. At work here are frequently radically different philosophical ontologies that propose alternative ways to understand how subjects are recruited to, and liberated from, power.

Radical Politics Without Hegemony

I've argued that hegemony's model of power is, broadly speaking, one of state-building – a process of organizing and connecting different groups and forces across a terrain of relatively open relations, rather than fixating on a single site alone. Although they differ on how that model is extended, theorists of hegemonic politics tend to understand it as a process of 'horizontal' expansion whereby the activity of making and sustaining strategic connections is given prominence over a static, ruling centre. But the ruling centre never quite disappears: hegemony still alerts us to some kind of 'vertical' ordering principle, institution, or agent that connects its different components. This reflects the Gramscian origins of many recent uses of hegemony, emerging as it did in a new era of mass politics when sovereign states became increasingly reliant on integrating their populations, rather than coercively subduing them.

For a number of radical critics, hegemony retains a statist logic that conceives politics, at least implicitly, in terms of projects of unification around a privileged centre. Even if that centre is rarely the exclusive focus of attention, or is necessarily modified by the way it articulates with others, hegemonic strategies nonetheless presuppose that its different branches ought to meet at some privileged point that confers on them a commonality. For Gramsci, that centre was the state, or, alternatively, the party through which a social class would assemble a national-popular 'collective will'. For later Marxists applying hegemony to the analysis of the capitalist state, Thatcherism, populism, or international politics, the centre was a class project or a dominant popular narrative. Even radical democrats, who dispute the necessity of a class as the centre of hegemony, still underscore the leading antagonism or 'empty signifier' through which all other struggles coalesce. Similarly, neo-Gramscians in IR highlight the organized 'bloc' of social forces (states, classes, and transnational institutions) and the ideological projects that secure international hegemony. The strategic dimension of hegemonic politics thus makes sense only in light of some organizing centre that orders the relations among its diverse components.

The concern of hegemony's contemporary critics is that an account of power based on the model of state-building will reproduce an analysis and a politics that is authoritarian. If hegemony is the ultimate context of politics, then no alternative politics will be taken seriously. Or, to put it another way, if we can only 'see like a state', then we will be condemned to imagine only a state-like politics. That means we will settle for understanding power as necessarily *tending towards* (if not actually achieving) the recruitment of subjects to a hierarchical structure, even though we acknowledge the unavoidable instability and openness of such structures. A leading group, institution, or principle will then be treated as a 'sovereign', a unifying 'master', even if it remains an empty fiction never finally incarnated. Hegemonic analysis, it might be argued, may dwell on the spatial expansion of power, but it remains implicitly wedded to the principle that political power is, or should be, unitary.

This is a problem raised particularly by theorists in the anarchist tradition who hold a principled objection to any politics seeking to aggregate collective social and political struggles into a single project. In his revealingly titled *Gramsci is Dead*, for example, Richard Day (2005) decries Post-Marxists who proclaim their commitment to plurality and difference. Hegemony, he argues, even in its radical democratic form, relies upon a 'logic of representation' that, like the liberalism it claims to supersede, is essentially statist: 'The expected outcome of the representation of a situation of inequality or lack of rights is *recognition* of the oppressed identity by the state apparatus' (2005: 75; italics in the original). The purpose of unifying different subordinate groups is to 'integrate' them, to make the supposedly 'benevolent' hegemonic order the privileged medium of their desires for emancipation. That, in his view, can only reproduce the authoritarian logic of subordination to a dominant master that corrupts most revolutionary projects of emancipation. 'To be hegemonized', Day underlines, means '*to be unable to rule oneself*' (2005: 47; italics in the original).

Similarly, Saul Newman's 'post-anarchist' political philosophy offers a theoretical critique of any absolute ordering principle – or *arché* – for thinking political power (Newman 2016). Such a principle is precisely what sovereign states and their rivals *want* people to endorse, disavowing the intrinsically diffuse and un-masterable nature of power. Seeking an alternative version of the same – however militant or pluralistic – is, therefore, hardly an advance. Indeed, contemporary anti-globalization and anti-capitalist struggles, for many anarchist thinkers, are evidence that a new, self-organized, and divergent form of radical politics is emergent. They frequently highlight the 1999 WTO protests in Seattle; the various Occupy movements around the world; the World Social Forum initiated in Porto Alegre, Brazil in 2001; the anti-austerity 'Indignados' movement in Spain from 2011; or the Taksim Gezi Park protests against urban development in Istanbul in 2013. In these, Newman finds affirmation not of hegemonic unity but, rather, of 'autonomy'. That is: 'seeking to transform the immediate situation and relationships that one finds oneself in, without necessarily seeing these actions and transformations as leading up to the great Social Revolution, and without measuring their success or failure in these terms' (2016: 12). There is, he argues, 'no Project of projects that determines all the others', and so we should beware any (hegemonic) politics that declares otherwise.

It is false to accuse Post-Marxist radical democrats and other neo-Gramscians of being advocates of an openly statist or authoritarian politics. But these critics highlight a significant point about how hegemony encourages a certain way of imagining political relations. What are often obscured or diminished by a hegemonic perspective are alternative modes of conceptualizing politics that are irreducible to organized strategies to unify blocs of support or generate collective wills. Radical activism and forms of protest and rebellion such as those listed above appear to instantiate singular, autonomous interventions that cannot be subsumed under any one overarching project (Graeber 2002). While certainly not all radical political theorists subscribe to anarchism or see these movements as a prototype for a new era of activism, the pluralistic and libertarian spirit they evoke nonetheless informs many strands of contemporary cultural and political theory today, particularly those opposed to the Marxist or Leninist tradition. Let us briefly review how they conceptualize politics differently, according to our three dimensions of hegemony.

Power and Ontology

Underlying different attitudes towards hegemony are contrasting philosophical ontologies. 'Ontology' concerns the character of being as such – the fundamental nature of things that exist. For the most part, contemporary radical thinkers reject ontologies that assert some eternal, positive 'ground' to all being. They refuse the idea that the basic structures of reality can be inferred from any universal principle, be it God, Nature, or Reason. Instead, they subscribe to a 'post-foundational' ontology for which there is no positive, self-sustaining principle to which all particular beings must automatically be referred. Indeed, it is precisely the *absence* of any 'essential' ordering principle that makes radical politics possible in the first place. Social relations are fundamentally open-ended and can be refashioned *because* they do not conform by necessity to any pre-given principle – or 'onto-theology' (Marchart 2007). But how this ground-lessness is manifest politically has drawn opposed positions and, with them, opposed views on the philosophical meaning and practical significance of hegemony.

We saw in chapter 4 how Laclau and Mouffe's poststructur-alist reconstruction of hegemony involves radical negativity, or antagonism. Hegemonic alliances, they argue, coalesce around encompassing conflicts that are perceived to pose a common existential threat. It is that negation – rather than some fully positive identity – that supplies the unifying point of reference for different demands. Following psychoanalyst Jacques Lacan, that approach is sometimes referred to as an 'ontology of lack' – the absence of completeness in social identities provides the motivation to identify an external antagonist – a shared source of incompleteness, such as an enemy or a claim of injustice (Marchart 2005). No positive entity such as class, or economic structure, automatically propels people into a common political project, only the contingent 'articulation' of their demands, which may form around *any* principle that is regarded as under threat (such as nationhood, freedom, justice, and so on). The foundation of hegemony, therefore, is not a positive quality but a negative one (an 'absent presence'), whose content remains histori-cally contingent, and hence perpetually revisable. Laclau and Mouffe's ontology of lack involves a hegemonic logic in which one political identity stands-in to fix 'partially' reality's intrinsic openness by granting disparate groups a temporary equivalence via some absent quality.

By contrast, other post-foundationalists appeal to what has been described as an 'ontology of abundance' (see Tønder and Thomassen 2005). Rather than a negative ground, they insist on the abundance of positivity. That is, reality consists fundamentally in creative forces that constantly *exceed* the contingent forms they take, overflowing them and recreating themselves in new ways. The inspirational figures here are Gilles Deleuze and Félix Guattari, whose vitalistic philosophy proposed just such an ontology of excess (Deleuze and Guattari 2013). This underscored a principle of perpetual 'becoming' – a movement of differentiation that constantly transgresses fixity – and it has been influential on more recent 'new materialist' philosophies (see Coole and Frost 2010; Connolly 2011). For Deleuze and Guattari, domination arises from obstacles to the creative movement, or 'rhizomatic' activity, of social 'desire', which perpetually expands and transforms in an uncontrolled fashion. They regard various social processes and forms of domination as practices of spatial 'territorialization' – that is, an imposition of rigid hierarchical patterns on natural, social, and psychical processes, aiming to stabilize power at the expense of mobility and 'flow'. This is the basis of Deleuze and Guattari's (essentially anarchistic) critique of capitalism, which they see as a system of territorialization and stratification that represses creativity. Rather than forming into blocs around negativity and prohibition, power is intrinsically dynamic and creative, constrained only by modes of thought and practice that try to capture its movement and impose on it rigid boundaries and limited direction.

Deleuze and Guattari's 'geo-physical language', Gilbert reminds us, is very far 'from a vocabulary that would contain concepts like hegemony' (2008: 147–8). Hegemony, for Laclau and Mouffe, is employed to describe a relative stabilization of social relations and identities – where 'discursive articulations' involve social compromises around a privileged antagonism. Deleuze and Guattari, however, see stabilization not as the consequence of conscious leadership but as a congeries of 'psycho-socio-physical' factors that are irreducible to political agency or conscious decisions. They invite exploration of the 'micro-level' processes and dynamic, divergent cultural configurations at work beneath, and therefore conditioning, 'macro-level' political calculations. This perspective offers insight into how resistant and transgressive activities are 'immanent' to forms of social domination – that is, emerging and undoing order from within.

Ontologies of abundance are more inclined to describe power and domination in part-natural, part-machinic forms and processes driven by their own autonomous, internal forces, than in terms of language and human agency. While the latter are not irrelevant, they are treated as responses to emergent energies and counter-forces that are self-organizing and independent of authoritative control. Power, as Lash summarizes it, is here understood as *potentiality* rather than a fixed quantity of force held in a single place – it is never fully spent but constantly seeks to reinvent itself, evading its blockages and transforming all things around it (Lash 2007: 59). This rather abstract conception has enabled theorists to tune in to deep variations and potentialities beneath institutional forms and discursive announcements, highlighting subtle differences and divergent possibilities. Thus, Willam Connolly (borrowing from Deleuze and Guattari) talks of neo-liberal capitalism not merely as a class-based structure of power, but, rather, as a 'global resonance machine': 'a cluster of energized elements of multiple types that enter into loose, re-enforcing conjugations as the whole complex both consolidates and continues to morph' (Connolly 2011: 135). Although certain agents may make an appearance in this machinic metaphor, what propels it is not some consciously organized force with a vision of social order. Indeed, the most disturbing aspect of it is that no one is in charge; no hegemonic state or strategy really commands the process.

Likewise, Hardt and Negri's (2000) popular explication of a new global 'Empire' describes a form of capitalism built on ever-expanding economic and communicative flows without any guiding centre. This expanding Empire is itself the outcome of former struggles and resistance by workers, whose international solidarity once sought to identify an 'outside' (either within or beyond the nation state) from which to limit capitalism and its effects. But now capitalism works not by disciplinary mechanisms, but through forms of control that 'directly organize the brains (in communication systems, information networks, etc.) and bodies (in welfare systems, monitored activities, etc.)' (2000: 23). No longer is there any conceivable outside; global capitalism dominates by extensively 'deterritorializing flows' (i.e., dissolving social and material barriers) such that any 'local' resistances merely 'feed into and support the development of the capitalist imperial machine' (2000: 45).

For these theorists, contingent struggles for hegemony are not the ultimate context of politics but, rather, something that may occur, at various levels, within the largely unpredictable, disorderly matrix of 'assemblages', 'machines', and 'territorialized' spaces inside which they try to carve out certain possibilities. If anything, hegemony is what the bad guys do – trying to fix and control, align and discipline individuals, society, and nature according to illusory 'transcendent' principles that assert mastery over our desires. But such strategies never exhaust the wider horizon of possibilities, so there is little point in magnifying their significance. At worst, hegemony implies – mistakenly in their view – that relations of power and domination are the outcome of some self-aware controlling agent external to this matrix. Theorists of abundance understand political struggles as immanent to relations of power – that is, forms of resistance arising from *within* the rich complex of energies and forces, and not via a 'transcendent' principle projected beyond them. Any kind of liberation turns not on the global negation and substitution of some identified dominant principle, but on its internal subversion, or 'reassemblage', and the affirmation of multiple, alternative possibilities. As we will see, this conception of power has implications for the other two dimensions of hegemony.

Affective Subjectivity

As we noted, theorists of hegemony typically highlight the role of subjects giving their assent to leading agents and ideas. That is the basis of their emphasis on forms of culture, ideology, or discourse as mechanisms to bind individuals and groups to certain 'common-sense' attitudes and arguments. But such mechanisms are sufficiently open-ended to allow for different articulations and inflections. Struggles for hegemony are therefore viewed, broadly, as passionate contests over meaning and identity, which erupt on the terrain of culture, even when they are connected to material relations and practices.

However, many contemporary theorists see power as operative primarily *through* subjectivity, not in dialogue with it: 'less a question of cognitive judgements and more a question of *being*', as Lash (2007: 58) puts it. That is to say, it is no longer what you think that matters but what you *are* in the global network of flows, mobility, and speed that characterizes contemporary power relations. Power works as a form of 'subjectification', subtly fashioning the subject by influencing it beneath its conscious capacities. Here the work of Foucault has been decisive, particularly his later work on 'bio-politics' and neo-liberal forms of 'governmentality' (Foucault 2008). In that work, the conforming subject is seen as something generated through rationalities and practices of freedom that incite and 'normalize' the individual *from within* as a self-governing agent. The liberal state, for example, does not so much impose its authority as rule by shaping the conduct of subjects from a distance, inciting them to regulate their own behaviours and desires as a matter of instinct rather than belief (see Dean 1999). Forms of population control, statistical management, classification and separation of 'healthy' and 'unhealthy' bodies, evocations of 'mindful' self-management, etc., do not 'repress' the individual's freedom but, rather, guide its behaviour and align its choices to outcomes geared towards enhancing its vitality. That type of control over the management of life and the space of individual choice – which is especially amplified in neo-liberal orders where market freedom is aggressively guided – constitutes subjects from the inside, as it were. It is not about persuasion or a hegemonic negotiation to 'win over' subjects, as if they were constituted prior to their guidance and regulation. These techniques are applied in the name of freedom itself. In such regimes, consent and coercion can barely be distinguished at all – the subject's freedom *is* the medium of control since it remains within predetermined parameters that function at the most minimal level of existence. The supposedly 'private' world of the citizen is increasingly subject to techniques of measurement, surveillance, and data-gathering that make its intimate activities (its consumer choices, its forms of enjoyment and leisure, its route to work) available for public regulation and corporate capture (see Davies 2018).

Contra theorists of hegemony, then, this strand of thinking argues that contemporary power rules less like a state trying to sustain a coalition of groups and interests through arguments and narratives, and more like an invasive network, without a guiding agent, that captures subjects and subdues them beyond any single, visible location. As Newman puts it: 'The Master we obey is an invisible one, and in many ways only a creation of our own obedience, yet we nonetheless obey it as though it were absolute' (2016: 23). Described here is a form of power that is 'totalitarian' in scope, working through people's daily experience but largely oblivious to the content of their demands. Attention to aspects of subjective capture therefore focus on affective and material processes that act upon the body, stimulating automatic responses, rather than through symbols and discourse alone (see Massumi 1995; Angerer 2015). Multiple, micro-level processes work *immediately* in and across bodies as they encounter technologies and are, thereby, inserted into wider circuits of power. For neo-liberal forms of government, what registers is not what we think but how we *perform* our feelings and reactions, since joy, outrage, or even indifference are sufficient to communicate our 'thoughtless' consuming and voting preferences and render us amenable to apparatuses of control (Lash 2007: 66).

What transpires for radical politics from this attention to the affective and corporeal layers of subjectivity is not the prospect of rearticulating 'demands' to a new hegemonic principle but, rather, exploring how alternative, 'fugitive', and inventive forms of cooperation might emerge beneath processes of subjectification (Day 2005: 80–8). As Lash surmises, this 'is an "exit" not a "voice" strategy', inviting a refusal to be captured rather than a negotiation over how much domination might be endured (2007: 67). It means looking to the 're-assemblage' of identity around new forms of life, as well as withdrawal from invasive control. Deleuzean-influenced currents of thinking are particularly focused on creative reinventions of subjectivity – or what Foucault called the 'arts of the self' – at a micro-level, which by-pass or subvert ingrained habits of thought and practice. For example, Connolly argues that philosophers 'tend to give too much self-sufficiency to consciousness and to limit thinking too much to the discovery of knowledge' (2002: 65). Instead, he suggests, we need to explore 'lower levels' of affective thinking that are creative, mobile, beyond conscious control, and receptive to corporeal sensations that are as yet unmapped. 'There is much more to thinking than argument', he underlines (2002: 74). To develop new forms of subjectivity means experimenting with experience – welcoming and engaging unfamiliar, intense, and provocative sensations that, at the macro-level of moral discourse, we are often discouraged from accessing. It is at the material level of affects and bodily practices that subjects are available for transformation and inscription into new, liberating modes of thought and being.

Activist currents of radical thought take even further this idea of the affectively constituted subject. Hardt and Negri have made the case for a whole new collective identity, emergent within what they see as the 'biopolitical' paradigm of global Empire. The expansion of so-called 'immaterial labour' (cultural and informational work, such as digital and media services, where workers are largely self-managing), global flows of trade, and networked communications has, in their view, generated a 'new proletariat' whose brains and bodies are now the medium of control. Paradoxically, it is the global system's reliance on the bodies and affects of 'nearly all of humanity' (2000: 43) that makes possible a new collective subject that they call 'the multitude' (Hardt and Negri 2005). This subject is comprised of a multiplicity of struggles for collective resistance and autonomy worldwide, forming 'a constituent counterpower that emerges from within Empire' to resist its invasive control (2000: 59). Hardt and Negri claim that 'the model of the horizontal articulation of struggles ... is no longer adequate' for global anti-capitalist struggles (2000: 57). What unifies the multitude is not 'resemblances' forged in the shared space of the factory, for instance, but differences – that is, a common distinctiveness or 'singularity' that is always particular to the contexts in which resistance emerges.

Where Hardt and Negri reinvent the Marxist idea of the proletariat as a global anti-capitalist subject, Newman's post-anarchist project endorses a more fractured sense of radical subjectivity. Newman views struggles for autonomy as the formation of distinct singularities, but not in the form of identification with 'the people' or even a multitude. For him, pervasive control of individuals invites an 'insurrectionary' refusal, a rebellious and spontaneous 'dis-identification' with power in order to pursue a variety of alternative ways of living outside the scope of any type of 'sovereign politics' (2016: 28–32). To truly escape affective integration into global capitalism, continues Newman, radical subjects can only function as particular instances of what, borrowing from Giorgio Agamben, he calls 'destituent power' (Newman 2017) – that is, autonomous struggles with no predefined telos, agendas, or demands aimed at connecting to all other struggles.

Ethics of Commitment

Already we can see that a non-hegemonic radical politics tends to emphasize leaderless contests and affective intensities over broader strategies and alliances. This connects to an ethical attitude that – to varying degrees, as we have seen – affirms the assertion of difference and the uniqueness of intense commitment over uniformity. That is not to say there is *no* acknowledgement of commonality across different struggles. But, for this broad strand of political thinking, the hegemonic aggregation of demands and identities is directly equated with domination because it appears to subsume the particularity of autonomy under an abstract, universal form. 'Leadership' implies submission to a group identity, and therefore suggests a diminution of opportunities for subjects to resist control or reinvent themselves.

For some theorists, of course, radical politics requires precisely that kind of leadership – a renewed 'Modern Prince' or a revolutionary Communist Party is exactly what is needed to overcome the fragmentation of contemporary anti-capitalist struggles and the obsessive, self-defeating paranoia of 'identity politics' (Sanbonmatsu 2004; Dean 2016). To be fair, Laclau and Mouffe's approach to hegemony has *never* affirmed anything remotely like a leading party or a formal organization. In their critique of the 'radical Jacobin imaginary', a democratic hegemony should be based on the principle of pluralism and refuse to collapse different emancipatory demands into a homogeneous identity. Mouffe's arguments about an 'agonistic' public sphere of adversaries further underscores this point. A radical democratic politics, she insists, must embrace the potential for conflict and hostility because its unity is not enforceable on the basis of a 'thick' consensus (Wenman 2013). Nonetheless, for some, Laclau and Mouffe's project for a left hegemony still remains focused on a 'spectral body of the People' filling the empty place of sovereign power (Newman 2016: 134).

For that reason, hegemony's radical critics see in the notion of hegemony a potential for authoritarianism that threatens the capacity for subjects to emancipate themselves, either individually or collectively. Any ethical dimension therefore ought to affirm a commitment to creative self-invention in the process of emancipation. Connolly's defence of pluralism, for example, goes way beyond the narrow liberal view of interest-group pluralism as a model of political order. He advocates a more radical 'ethos of pluralization', understood as an invitation to ever-expanding types of difference (Connolly 1995, 2005). In support of this, he endorses an ethics of 'agonistic respect' and 'generosity' among cultural and political opponents. To cultivate a rich democratic life, what is necessary is not so much a single enemy, or antagonist, as a 'public ethos' that encourages 'intracultural' exploration and engagement with the 'layered texture of being' (2002: 138) – or a radically diverse and inventive cultural community. Similarly, Jane Bennett makes the case for a 'post-human' radical democracy, understood not as a space simply for humans and their arguments but as a 'parliament of things' where humans and non-humans (such as the natural and built environment, animals, technology) are recognized as co-participants in the fostering of an entangled common world (Bennett 2005).

More radical, (post-)anarchist theorists tend to go even further in advocating a militant, anti-authoritarian politics of direct action. Such activism prizes an ethic of commitment through a participatory, sometimes 'pre-figurative' politics aimed at generating alternative types of self-government outside the reach of formal institutions. Day (2005: 89) calls this a 'politics of the act', which means 'giving up' on seeking validation from structures of domination.

Traditional democratic representational politics, it has been argued, is increasingly regarded by citizens as ineffective and elitist, reliant on bureaucratic and instrumentalist habits that separate ordinary people from matters of deep public concern (Tormey 2015). Instead, many kinds of radical activism now look to a democratic politics that is instant, informal, involving temporary 'networks of affinity' and 'insurgent' mobilizations on the street rather than lengthy debates, formal lobbying, or committee meetings. Here, asserting the freedom to govern oneself, and hence one's independence from formal power structures and norms, rather than any horizontal extension or organized leadership, is the motivating principle. As Newman presents it, an 'insurrectionary' politics such as this constitutes a type of 'agonistic anarchism', which he claims is a 'much more fundamental form of agonism', in which conflict is primarily between diverse projects of self-organization and the assertion of state sovereignty (Newman 2016: 135). This politics 'resituates the dimension of "the political" from the ontological order of the state ... to the dissenting world of contemporary practices and movements which seek autonomy from this order' (2016: 135–6).

A Moment for Strategy

Clearly, then, a substantial swathe of radical political thinking is deeply suspicious of any positive reference to hegemony, and has alternative philosophical paradigms and models of politics and ethics to offer in its stead. Hegemony is viewed as an 'analogue' concept in a digital age, or (to switch metaphors) a heavy-footed mammoth unable to adapt to a world of speed and flight. The point of radical politics, they argue, can only be to overcome hegemony. Emancipation today is about subverting the grip of neo-liberal capitalism over every aspect of life, freeing up desires to reinvent selfhood, propelled by a militant sense of commitment and a refusal to be captured by power. There are, as we have seen, stronger and weaker versions of this outlook, but they all circle around a similar suspicion of hegemony.

It should be noted that Laclau and Mouffe – whose work on contemporary hegemonic politics is often the target of this critical reception – have themselves disputed the critical claims made about the content and orientation of their thinking. Much of their response involves reasserting the importance of strategy to political action. Mouffe, for example, argues that neo-liberal capitalism is not a homogeneous and self-expanding phenomenon but, rather, a process whose imperatives are contingently assembled. Although many aspects of neo-liberal institutions and cultures are now deeply embedded, they often arrive through contest and strategy, and meet popular challenge. Far from being a fully decentred network of smooth flows, 'global space' remains unevenly organized around nation states, regions, and cities, not all of which are equivalent locations in the vast neo-liberal Empire. These serve as 'nodal' points in both neo-liberal expansion and resistance, even if they are no longer as powerful as they once were (Mouffe 2005: 107–15). Popular resistance and wider public attitudes remain shaped by a sense of 'the common' forged at these locations. Both Laclau and Mouffe, therefore, dispute the idea that any new radical political consciousness might arrive without strategic articulation – and they are particularly scathing about Hardt and Negri's romantic vision of a 'multitude' emerging 'immanently' without equivalences and differences across different struggles being actively made. Rather than a multiplicity of independent, 'vertical' protests spontaneously cohering in their opposition to Empire, a collective political subject requires deliberate selection to make a 'horizontal' connection (Laclau 2001: 7–9). That means, in their view, finding a common antagonism and, consequently, a politics of hegemony.

This point about strategy is an important one, even for those who adopt an ontology of abundance and the analyses associated with it. Without attention to the strategic nature of power, it becomes difficult to see domination as involving anything other than *total* submission, and resistance to power as any more than spontaneous, episodic 'experiments' and confrontations with no impact on each other. One of the hazards of an 'anti-neoliberal' discourse that perpetually reiterates contemporary capitalism's inherent and pervasive iniquities is that it describes an inexorable, totalizing force that can only be confronted as a whole (see Gilbert 2008: 208–9). That may mirror the logic of neo-liberal reason, but it tends to present such a logic as if it were instantiated equally in any and every instance. The danger is that either resistance is felt to be futile – since it can't achieve much, given the odds – or it has to involve a wholesale re-figuration of the self, often with a tendency to fetishize direct action as evidence of one's 'pure' commitment. But such commitment – whether to tackle neo-liberalism or even to withdraw self-consciously from its clutches – is difficult to imagine for most people, even all activists. If radical opposition is to be effective beyond discrete instances of confrontation, then coordination and conversation among different localities and experiences is necessary.

Indeed, that is precisely what Jeremy Gilbert (2008) proposes in one of few efforts at a synthesis of the pro- and anti-hegemonic positions: a 'counter-hegemonic' orientation that would respect the many different kinds of struggles against neo-liberal measures around the world, their unique local concerns and ethical objectives, but which *also* aims at generating a common discourse, if only minimally organized around opposition to neo-liberalism. Gilbert acknowledges the insights of Deleuzian analysis, particularly for encouraging creative responses to the ways in which globalization simultaneously coerces and persuades. And he accepts the anarchist observation that traditional revolutionary movements have tended to suppress creativity and autonomy, and that strategic choices often end up with compromises with power. But, without *any* strategic orientation – that is, without persuading others by developing forms of leadership, sharing knowledge, building alliances, and identifying shared antagonists – it is impossible to progress beyond isolated tactics of subversion and intermittent spectacles of unrest. Hegemony, he argues, is not equivalent to domination; leadership 'does not necessarily imply the imposition of a singular will on others' (2008: 220). Counter-hegemony can do without a hierarchical party or a model of a state, but its strategy should involve ongoing dialogue through social forums, formulating charters with common principles, social experiments with temporary alliances at different scales

among different activist groups, as well as consideration
as to how anti-capitalism might include those who are not
full-time activists.

> A political movement which really wants to effect any kind
> of social change has to find a way to include, to attract, to
> resonate with such people. Inclusion in this sense does not
> necessarily involve taking a direct part in political activity,
> but a more general sharing of attitudes, assumptions and
> responses – an affective exchange – which can translate into
> active political support at times of real crisis and can become
> a basis for a generalised militancy which does not depend
> upon the presence of militants for its success. (2008: 233)

What Gilbert sketches here is reminiscent of Gramsci's 'war
of position' – that is, the cultivation of a broad, cultural
leadership that draws upon various creative responses to
contemporary capitalism so as to sustain alliances and
engage ordinary people, while disavowing the hierarchy
and instrumentalism typical of a revolutionary movement.
However realistic such a project might be, it does underline
the continued significance of strategy as a vital moment in the
radical political imaginary.

Despite efforts to analyse contemporary political struggles
outside of a framework of hegemony, then, there might yet
be reasonable grounds to retain the concept. The defence
of hegemony made by Gilbert and others is not undertaken
with the intent of making it the defining horizon of any and
all radical politics, as Laclau and Mouffe sometimes appear
to claim. It is possible to explore the strategic expansion of
economic and political power, and the building of resistance
to it, without insisting exclusively on some 'sovereign' centre
that does the unifying. Hegemony might be conceived as a
strategic moment in most political formations – a temporary
conjoining of institutions and ideas so as to consolidate
and expand certain initiatives – without neglecting the
wider complexity and inventiveness of power. That theorists
increasingly pay more attention to the divergent and singular
possibilities operative underneath or at the margins of
power does not mean that strategic moments do not ever
occur. They may not all arrive as 'national-popular' projects
driven by clearly defined movements, parties, or states. In

a post-sovereign age, where 'flows of communications and finance' (Lash 2007: 66) increasingly shape the international field, hegemonic leadership is less likely to be as decisive or enduring as earlier theories of hegemony imagined. But strategic moments are still necessary and, as a consequence, hegemony continues to deserve a place in the lexicon of radical political analysis.

Conclusion

Although it has now achieved a degree of respectability through widespread use, hegemony has always been something of a risky concept. It presents a model of power whose boundaries are inherently ambiguous – where is the line that separates leadership from domination, force from consent, state from civil society? These questions invite judgement as much as objectivity. Analyses of hegemony often urge us to glimpse a moving target rather than locate a fixed, contoured object. Perhaps inevitably, that means the image we have is frequently more a blur than a crisp picture. Rather than 'neutrally' describing power, hegemony is an interpretive category concerned with how, collectively, people themselves 'build reality' by following the lead of certain agents and inhabiting their ideas (Blakely 2020). Power and domination are therefore inseparable from the ways in which social meanings circulate and inflect popular ideas of what is possible or desirable. To examine and act on this terrain means judging the depth and strength of forms of 'influence', a phenomenon that is typically uneven and forever shifting.

Such ambiguity has been thought necessary, in part, because hegemony usually qualifies more rigid views about structures of power and domination. That was especially so as regards reductive forms of Marxism, against which the concept was revived in the twentieth century. Different approaches to hegemony have since applied the concept to other fields with varying emphases and in ways that acknowledge power's moving boundaries without, nonetheless, collapsing them entirely. At their best, these have produced nuanced, illuminating analyses that explore the dynamic interaction of different agents and forces, and the social compromises that simultaneously hold them all together and apart. At worst, however, they can incline towards a reductive homogenization that collapses almost everything into an amorphous structure of domination. Similarly, hegemony can inspire a politics aimed at the skilful coordination and unification of multiple interests and aspirations, which – if only at certain, decisive moments – might hold sway in wider configurations of power. But it can also invite a narrow, hierarchical, and statist image of politics that equates it with the unchecked authority of a leader, ideology, or interest.

As we have seen in this chapter, not everyone is prepared to accept the risks that hegemony runs, either analytically or politically. As a concept that came into general usage as nation states sought to consolidate their control both internally and internationally, hegemony's contrasting accents mirror the ambiguous nature of modern power itself – potentially liberating but also oppressive, unifying but also exclusionary. Other modalities – and so other accounts – of power have emerged that are not always amenable to a hegemonic framework. That is particularly so in relation to the creative movement identified in new forms of power and its resistance. To those who reason from such movement, hegemony's institutional references, theoretical frames, or conceptual logic may seem anachronistic, and its ambiguities dangerously deceptive.

Yet, as we noted, those analyses also assume some capacity for strategy and coordination, even if they do not foreground these as major themes for radical politics and analysis. Which is to say that, after we acknowledge the limitations of hegemony as a framework for conceptualizing and practising politics, nonetheless its risks may still be worth taking. Instead of talking about the 'end' of hegemony, we would be better off reflecting on what new questions it *can* help us to ask, particularly at a moment when nation states and national cultures function less and less effectively as vehicles for exercising social and political leadership. As long as power seeks consent, and consent continues to be a source of contest, hegemony is likely to remain a vital resource for negotiating the strategic conditions of politics.

References

Almond, S. and Verba, G. A. (1965) *The Civic Culture: Political Attitudes and Democracy in Five Nations*. New York: Little, Brown & Co.

Althusser, L. (1969) *For Marx*. London: Penguin.

Althusser, L. (1971) 'Ideology and ideological state apparatuses (Notes towards an investigation)' in *Lenin and Philosophy and Other Essays*. London: New Left Books.

Althusser, L. and Balibar, E. (1970) *Reading Capital*. London: New Left Books.

Anderson, P. (1976–7) 'The antimonies of Antonio Gramsci', *New Left Review* 100: 5–78.

Anderson, P. (1979) *Considerations on Western Marxism*. London: Verso.

Anderson, P. (1992) *English Questions*. London: Verso.

Anderson, P. (2016) *The H-Word: The Peripeteia of Hegemony*. London: Verso.

Angerer, M.-L. (2015) *Desire after Affect*. London: Rowman & Littlefield.

Archibugi, D. (2008) *The Global Commonwealth of Citizens: Toward Cosmopolitan Democracy*. Princeton University Press.

Artz, L. and Murphy, B. O. (2000) *Cultural Hegemony in the United States*. London: Sage.

Ashley, R. K. (1988) 'Untying the sovereign state: A double reading of the anarchy problematique', *Millennium* 17(2): 227–62.

Augelli, E. and Murphy, C. (1988) *America's Quest for Supremacy and the Third World: An Essay in Gramscian Analysis*. London: Continuum.

Ball, T. (1975) 'Power, causation and explanation', *Polity* 8(2): 189–214.

Beasley-Murray, J. (2010) *Posthegemony: Political Theory and Latin America*. London: University of Minnesota Press.

Beetham, D. (2013) *The Legitimation of Power*, 2nd edition. Basingstoke: Palgrave.

Bell, D. (2000) *The End of Ideology: On the Exhaustion of Political Ideas in the Fifties*, 5th edition. Cambridge, MA: Harvard University Press.

Bellamy, R. (1987) *Modern Italian Social Theory: Ideology and Politics from Pareto to the Present*. Cambridge: Polity.

Bellamy, R. (1990). 'Gramsci, Croce and the Italian political tradition', *History of Political Thought* 11(2): 313–37.

Bellamy, R. and Schecter, D. (1993) *Gramsci and the Italian State*. Manchester University Press.

Bennett, J. (2005) 'In parliament with things' in L. Tønder and L. Thomassen (eds.) *Radical Democracy: Politics Between Abundance and Lack*. Manchester University Press.

Bieler, A., Bruff, I., and Morton, A. D. (2015) 'Gramsci and "the International": Past, present and future' in D. McNally (ed.) *Antonio Gramsci*. Basingstoke: Palgrave Macmillan.

Blakely, J. (2020) *We Built Reality: How Social Science Infiltrated Culture, Politics, and Power*. Oxford University Press.

Bloomfield, R. (1977) *Class, Hegemony and Party: Lectures from the Communist University of London*. London: Lawrence & Wishart.

Bobbio, N. (1986) *Which Socialism? Marxism, Socialism and Democracy*. Cambridge: Polity.

Brenner, N. (2004) *New State Space: Urban Governance and the Rescaling of Statehood*. Oxford University Press.

Brenner, N. and Theodore, N. (eds.) (2002) *Spaces of Neoliberalism: Urban Restructuring in North America and Western Europe*. Oxford: Blackwell.

Bull, H. (2002) *The Anarchical Society: A Study of Order in World Politics*, 3rd edition. Basingstoke: Palgrave.

Burnham, P. (1991) 'Neo-Gramscian hegemony and the international order', *Capital & Class* 15(3): 73–93.

Butler, J., Laclau, E., and Žizek, S. (2000) *Contingency, Hegemony, Universality: Contemporary Dialogues on the Left*. London: Verso.

Castells, M. (2010) *The Rise of the Network Society*, 2nd edition. Oxford: Blackwell.

CCCS (Centre for Contemporary Cultural Studies) (ed.) (1977) *On Ideology*. London: Hutchinson.

Chandler, D. and Reid, J. (2016) *The Neoliberal Subject: Resilience, Adaptation and Vulnerability*. London: Rowman & Littlefield.

Chomsky, N. (2003) *Hegemony or Survival: America's Quest for Global Dominance*. London: Penguin.

Clark, I. (2009) 'Bringing hegemony back in: The United States and international order', *International Affairs* 85(1): 23–36.

Clark, I. (2011) *Hegemony in International Society*. Oxford University Press.

Clark, M. (1979) *Antonio Gramsci and the Revolution that Failed*. New Haven: Yale University Press.

Clark, M. (1984) *Modern Italy 1871–1982*. London: Longman.

Clegg, S. R. (1989) *Frameworks of Power*. London: Sage.

Connell, R. W. and Messerschmidt, J. W. (2005) 'Hegemonic masculinity: Rethinking the concept', *Gender & Society* 19(6): 829–59.

Connolly, W. E. (1995) *The Ethos of Pluralization*. London: University of Minnesota Press.

Connolly, W. E. (2002) *Neuropolitics: Thinking, Culture, Speed*. London: University of Minnesota Press.

Connolly, W. E. (2005) *Pluralism*. London: Duke University Press.

Connolly, W. E. (2011) *A World of Becoming*. London: Duke University Press.

Coole, D. and Frost, S. (eds.) (2010) *New Materialisms: Ontology, Agency, and Politics*. London: Duke University Press.

Cox, R. W. (1987) *Production, Power and World Order: Social Forces in the Making of History*. New York: Columbia University Press.

Cox, R. W. (1993) 'Gramsci, hegemony and international relations: An essay on method' in S. Gill (ed.) *Gramsci, Historical Materialism and International Relations*. Cambridge University Press.

Dahlberg, L. and Phelan, S. (2011) *Discourse Theory and Critical Media Politics*. Basingstoke: Palgrave Macmillan.

Dahlberg, L. and Siapera, E. (eds.) (2007) *Radical Democracy and the Internet: Interrogating Theory and Practice*. Basingstoke: Palgrave Macmillan.

Davidson, A. (1977) *Antonio Gramsci: Towards an Intellectual Biography*. London: Merlin.

Davies, M. (1999) *International Political Economy and Mass Communication in Chile: National Intellectuals and Transnational Hegemony*. Basingstoke: Macmillan.

Davies, W. (2018) *Nervous States: How Feeling Took Over the World*. London: Jonathan Cape.

Day, R. (2005) *Gramsci is Dead: Anarchist Currents in the Newest Social Movements*. London: Pluto.

Dean, J. (2016) *Crowds and Party*. London: Verso.

Dean, M. (1999) *Governmentality: Power and Rule in Modern Society*. London: Sage.

de la Torre, C. (2018) *Populisms: A Quick Emersion*. New York: Tibidabo.

Deleuze, G. and Guattari, F. (2013) *Anti-Oedipus: Capitalism and Schizophrenia*. London: Bloomsbury.

Derrida, J. (1978) *Writing and Difference*. London: Routledge.

Derrida, J. (1988) *Limited Inc*. Evanston: Northwestern University Press.

Dworkin, D. (1997) *Cultural Marxism in Postwar Britain: History, the New Left, and the Origins of Cultural Studies*. London: Duke University Press.

Elliott, G. (1987). *Althusser: The Detour of Theory*. London: Verso.

Errejón, I. and Mouffe, C. (2016) *Podemos: In the Name of the People*. London: Lawrence & Wishart.

Femia, J. V. (1981) *Gramsci's Political Thought: Hegemony, Consciousness, and the Revolutionary Process*. Oxford: Clarendon.

Femia, J. V. (1998) *The Machiavellian Legacy: Essays in Italian Political Thought*. Basingstoke: Palgrave Macmillan.

Femia, J. V. (2005) 'Gramsci, Machiavelli and international relations', *The Political Quarterly* 76(3): 341–9.

Ferguson, N. (2005) *Colossus: The Rise and Fall of the American Empire*. London: Penguin.

Fontana, B. (1993) *Hegemony and Power: On the Relation between Gramsci and Machiavelli*. London: University of Minnesota Press.

Forgacs, D. (1989) 'Gramsci and Marxism in Britain', *New Left Review* 176: 70–88.

Foucault, M. (1977) *Discipline and Punish: The Birth of the Prison*. New York: Vintage.

Foucault, M. (1978) *The History of Sexuality: An Introduction*. London: Penguin.

Foucault, M. (1980) 'Truth and power' in C. Gordon (ed.) *Power/Knowledge: Selected Interviews and Other Writings 1972–1977*. London: Harvester Wheatsheaf.

Foucault, M. (2008) *The Birth of Biopolitics: Lectures at the Collège de France 1978–1979*. Basingstoke: Palgrave Macmillan.

Gamble, A. (1994) *The Free Economy and the Strong State: The Politics of Thatcherism*, 2nd edition. Basingstoke: Palgrave.

Geras, N. (1987) 'Post-Marxism?' *New Left Review* 163: 40–82.

Germain, R. D. and Kenny, M. (1998) 'Engaging Gramsci: International relations theory and the new Gramscians', *Review of International Studies* 24(1): 3–21.

Giddens, A. (1991) *Modernity and Self-Identity: Self and Society in the Late Modern Age*. Cambridge: Polity.

Gilbert, J. (2008) *Anticapitalism and Culture: Radical Theory and Popular Politics*. Oxford: Berg.

Gill, S. (1990) *American Hegemony and the Trilateral Commission*. Cambridge University Press.

Gill, S. (ed.) (1993) *Gramsci, Historical Materialism and International Relations*. Cambridge University Press.

Gill, S. and Cutler, A. C. (eds.) (2015) *New Constitutionalism and World Order*. Cambridge University Press.

Gill, S. and Law, D. (1993) 'Global hegemony and the structural power of capital' in S. Gill (ed.) *Gramsci, Historical Materialism and International Relations*. Cambridge University Press.

Gilroy, P. (1992) *There Ain't No Black in the Union Jack: The Cultural Politics of Race and Nation*. London: Routledge.

Glynos, J. and Howarth, D. (2007) *Logics of Critical Explanation in Social and Political Theory*. Abingdon: Routledge.

Golding, S. (1992) *Gramsci's Democratic Theory: Contributions to a Post-Liberal Democracy*. London: University of Toronto.

Graeber, D. (2002) 'The new anarchists', *New Left Review* 13: 61–73.

Gramsci, A. (1971) *Selections from the Prison Notebooks*. London: Lawrence & Wishart.

Gramsci, A. (1977) *Selections from Political Writings, 1910–1920*. London: Lawrence & Wishart.

Gramsci, A. (1978) *Selections from Political Writings, 1921–1926*. London: Lawrence & Wishart.

Gramsci, A. (1995) *Further Selections from the Prison Notebooks*. London: Lawrence & Wishart.

Gray, J. (2009) *False Dawn: The Delusions of Global Capitalism*. London: Granta.

Gundle, S. (1995) 'The legacy of the Prison Notebooks: Gramsci, the PCI and Italian culture in the Cold War period' in C. Duggan and C. Wagstaff (eds.) *Italy in the Cold War: Politics, Culture and Society 1948–58*. Oxford: Berg.

Hall, S. (1986) 'Gramsci's relevance for the study of race and ethnicity', *Journal of Communication Enquiry* 10: 5–27.

Hall, S. (1988) *The Hard Road to Renewal: Thatcherism and the Crisis of the Left*. London: Verso.

Hall, S. (1998) 'The great moving nowhere show', *Marxism Today* (Special Issue): 9–14.

Hall, S. and Jacques, M. (eds.) (1983) *The Politics of Thatcherism*. London: Lawrence & Wishart.

Hall, S. and Jefferson, T. (eds.) (1975) *Resistance Through Rituals: Youth Sub-cultures in Post-War Britain*. London: Hutchinson.

Hall, S., Critcher, C., Jefferson, T., Clarke, J. and Roberts, B. (1978) *Policing the Crisis: Mugging, the State, and Law and Order*. London: Macmillan.

Hall, S., Lumley, R., and McLennan, G. (1977) 'Politics and ideology: Gramsci' in CCCS (ed.) *On Ideology*. London: Hutchinson.

Hardt, M. and Negri, A. (2000) *Empire*. Cambridge, MA: Harvard University Press.

Hardt, M. and Negri, A. (2005) *Multitude: War and Democracy in the Age of Empire*. London: Penguin.

Harris, D. (1992). *From Class Struggle to the Politics of Pleasure: The Effects of Gramscianism on Cultural Studies*. London: Routledge.

Harvey, D. (2005) *A Brief History of Neoliberalism*. Oxford University Press.

Haugaard, M., and Lentner, H. H. (eds.) (2006) *Hegemony and Power: Consensus and Coercion in Contemporary Politics*. Oxford: Lexington Books.

Hay, C. (1996) *Re-Stating Social and Political Change*. Buckingham: Open University Press.

Held, D. (1995) *Democracy and the Global Order: From the Modern State to Cosmopolitan Governance*. Cambridge: Polity.

Hesketh, C. (2019) 'A Gramscian conjuncture in Latin America? Reflections on violence, hegemony, and geographical difference', *Antipode* 51(5): 1474–94.

Hirst, P. and Thompson, G. (1999) *Globalization in Question*. Cambridge: Polity.

Hobbes, T. (1991) *Leviathan*. Cambridge University Press.

Holton, R. J. (1998) *Globalization and the Nation-State*. Basingstoke: Macmillan.

Howarth, D. (2000) *Discourse*. Buckingham: Open University Press.

Howarth, D. and Torfing, J. (eds.) (2005) *Discourse Theory in European Politics: Identity, Policy and Governance*. Basingstoke: Palgrave Macmillan.

Howarth, D., Norval, A. J., and Stavrakakis, Y. (eds.) (2000) *Discourse Theory and Political Analysis: Identities, Hegemonies and Social Change*. Manchester University Press.

Hunt, A. (ed.) (1980) *Marxism and Democracy*. London: Lawrence & Wishart.

Ikenbury, G. J. (2011) *Liberal Leviathan: The Origins, Crisis, and Transformations of the American World Order*. Princeton University Press.

Ives, P. (2004) *Language and Hegemony in Gramsci*. London: Pluto.

Jacobitti, E. E. (1981) *Revolutionary Humanism and Historicism in Modern Italy*. London: Yale University Press.

Jessop, B. (1990) *State Theory: Putting Capitalist States Back in their Place*. Cambridge: Polity.

Jessop, B. (2002) *The Future of the Capitalist State*. Cambridge: Polity.

Jessop, B. (2007) 'New Labour or the normalization of neo-liberalism', *British Politics* 2(3): 282–8.

Jessop, B. (2015) 'Margaret Thatcher and Thatcherism: Dead but not buried', *British Politics* 10(1): 16–30.

Jessop, B., Bonnett, K., Bromley, S. and Ling, T. (1984) 'Authoritarian populism, two nations, and Thatcherism', *New Left Review* 147: 32–60.

Jessop, B., Bonnett, K., Ling, T. and Bromley, S. (1988) *Thatcherism: A Tale of Two Nations*. Cambridge: Polity.

Joseph, J. (2002) *Hegemony: A Realist Analysis*. London: Routledge.

Judt, T. (2005) *Postwar: A History of Europe since 1945*. London: Vintage.

Kavanagh, D. (1994) *Consensus Politics: From Attlee to Major*, 2nd edition. London: Wiley.

Kenny, M. (1995) *The First New Left: British Intellectuals after Stalin*. London: Lawrence & Wishart.

Keohane, R. O. (1984) *After Hegemony: Cooperation and Discord in the World Political Economy*. Princeton University Press.

Lacan, J. (2006) *Écrits*. London: Norton & Co.

Lacan, J. (2007) *The Other Side of Psychoanalysis: The Seminar of Jacques Lacan Book XVII*. London: Norton & Co.

Lacan, J. (2013) 'The symbolic, the imaginary and the real' in *On the Names-of-the-Father*. Cambridge: Polity.

Laclau, E. (1977) *Politics and Ideology in Marxist Theory: Capitalism – Fascism – Populism*. London: Verso.

Laclau, E. (1990) *New Reflections on the Revolution of Our Time*. London: Verso.

Laclau, E. (1996) *Emancipation(s)*. London: Verso.

Laclau, E. (2001) 'Can immanence explain social struggles?' *diacritics* 31(4): 3–10.

Laclau, E. (2018) *On Populist Reason*. London: Verso.

Laclau, E. and Mouffe, C. (1985) *Hegemony and Socialist Strategy: Towards a Radical Democratic Politics*. London: Verso.

Laclau, E. and Mouffe, C. (1987) 'Post-Marxism without apologies', *New Left Review* 166: 79–106.

Lash, S. (2007) 'Power after hegemony: Cultural studies in mutation', *Theory, Culture and Society* 24(3): 55–78.

Lebow, R. N. and Kelly, R. (2001) 'Thucydides and hegemony: Athens and the United States', *Review of International Studies* 27(4): 593–609.

Lenin, V. I. (1992) *The State and Revolution*. London: Penguin.

Lenin, V. I. (2010) *Imperialism: The Highest Stage of Capitalism*. London: Penguin.

Lester, J. (2000) *Dialogue of Negation: Debates on Hegemony in Russia and the West*. London: Pluto.

Lyotard, J.-F. (1984) *The Postmodern Condition: A Report on Knowledge*. Manchester University Press.

Lyttelton, A. (1973) *The Seizure of Power: Fascism in Italy, 1919–1929*. London: Weidenfeld and Nicolson.

Machiavelli, N. (1988) *The Prince*. Cambridge University Press.

Marchart, O. (2005) 'The absence at the heart of presence: Radical democracy and the ontology of lack' in L. Tønder and L. Thomassen (eds.) *Radical Democracy: Politics Between Abundance and Lack*. Manchester University Press.

Marchart, O. (2007) *Post-Foundational Political Thought: Political Difference in Nancy, Lefort, Badiou and Laclau*. Edinburgh University Press.

Marx, K. and Engels, F. (1996) 'Manifesto of the Communist Party' in T. Carver (ed.) *Marx: Later Political Writings*. Cambridge University Press.

Massumi, B. (1995) 'The autonomy of affect', *Cultural Critique* 31 (Fall): 83–109.

McNally, M. (2015) 'Gramsci, the United Front Comintern and democratic strategy' in M. McNally (ed.) *Antonio Gramsci*. Basingstoke: Palgrave.

Meiksins-Wood, E. (1999) *The Retreat from Class: A New True Socialism?* London: Verso.

Miliband, R. (1973) *The State in Capitalist Society*. London: Quartet.

Miliband, R. (1977) *Marxism and Politics*. Oxford University Press.

Miliband, R., Panitch, L. and Saville, J. (eds.) (1987) *Conservatism in Britain and America: Rhetoric and Reality, Socialist Register 1987*. London: Merlin.

Mills, C. W. (2000) *The Power Elite*. Oxford University Press.

Moffitt, B. (2015) 'How to perform crisis: A model for understanding the key role of crisis in contemporary populism', *Government & Opposition* 50(2): 189–217.

Moffitt, B. (2020) *Populism*. Cambridge: Polity.

Morgan, P. (2003) *Fascism in Europe, 1914–1945*. Abingdon: Routledge.

Morgenthau, H. (1948) *Politics Among Nations: The Struggle for Power and Peace*. New York: Knopf.

Morton, A. D. (2003a) 'Historicizing Gramsci: Situating ideas in and beyond their context', *Review of International Political Economy* 10(1): 118–46.

Morton, A. D. (2003b) 'Social forces in the struggle over hegemony: Neo-Gramscian perspectives in International Political Economy', *Rethinking Marxism* 15(2): 153–79.

Morton, A. D. (2007) *Unravelling Gramsci: Hegemony and Passive Revolution in the Global Economy*. London: Pluto.

Mouffe, C. (1979) 'Hegemony and ideology in Gramsci' in C. Mouffe (ed.) *Gramsci and Marxist Theory*. London: Routledge & Kegan Paul.

Mouffe, C. (1993) *The Return of the Political*. London: Verso.

Mouffe, C. (2000) *The Democratic Paradox*. London: Verso.

Mouffe, C. (2005) *On the Political*. London: Routledge.

Mouffe, C. (2013) *Agonistics: Thinking the World Politically*. London: Verso.

Munck, R. P. (2013) *Rethinking Latin America: Development, Hegemony, and Social Transformation*. New York: Palgrave Macmillan.

Nagle, A. (2017) *Kill All Norms: Online Culture Wars from 4Chan and Tumblr to Trump and the Alt-Right*. Winchester: Zero Books.

Nairn, T. (1981) *The Breakup of Britain: Crisis and Neo-nationalism*, 2nd edition. London: Verso.

Newman, S. (2016) *Post-Anarchism*. Cambridge: Polity.

Newman, S. (2017) 'What is an insurrection? Destituent power and ontological anarchy in Agamben and Stirner', *Political Studies* 65(2): 284–99.

Norval, A. J. (1998) *Deconstructing Apartheid Discourse*. London: Verso.

Opratko, B. (2012) *Hegemonie: Politische Theorie nach Antonio Gramsci*. Münster: Westfälisches Dampfboot.

Poulantzas, N. (1973) *Political Power and Social Classes*. London: New Left Books.

Poulantzas, N. (1974) *Fascism and Dictatorship: The Third International and the Problem of Fascism*. London: Verso.

Poulantzas, N. (1978) *State, Power, Socialism*. London: Verso.

Poulantzas, N. (2008) *The Poulantzas Reader: Marxism, Law, and the State*. London: Verso.

Prentoulis, M. (2021) *Left Populism in Europe: Lessons from Jeremy Corbyn to Podemos*. London: Pluto.

Przybylowicz, D. (1990) 'Towards a feminist cultural criticism: Hegemony and modes of social division', *Cultural Critique* 14 (Winter): 259–301.

Robinson, W. I. (2005) 'Gramsci and globalization: From nation-state to transnational hegemony', *Critical Review of International Social and Political Philosophy* 8(4): 559–74.

Rosenberg, J. (1994) *The Empire of Civil Society: A Critique of the Realist Theory of International Relations*. London: Verso.

Rowe, W. and Schelling, V. (1991) *Memory and Modernity: Popular Culture in Latin America*. London: Verso.

Rupert, M. (1995) *Producing Hegemony: The Politics of Mass Production and American Global Power*. Cambridge University Press.

Rupert, M. (2000) *Ideologies of Globalisation: Contending Visions of a New World Order*. London: Routledge.

Rustin, M. (1987) 'Absolute voluntarism: Critique of a Post-Marxist concept of hegemony', *New German Critique* 43: 146–73.

Salem, S. (2020) *Anticolonial Afterlives in Egypt: The Politics of Hegemony*. Cambridge University Press.

Sanbonmatsu, J. (2004) *The Postmodern Prince: Critical Theory, Left Strategy, and the Making of a New Political Subject*. New York: Monthly Review Press.

Sassoon, A. S. (1987) *Gramsci's Politics*, 2nd edition. London: Hutchinson.

Sassoon, D. (1981) *The Strategy of the Italian Communist Party: From the Resistance to the Historic Compromise*. London: Pinter.

Sassoon, D. (1990) 'The role of the Italian Communist Party in the consolidation of parliamentary democracy in Italy' in G. Pridham (ed.) *Securing Democracy: Political Parties and Democratic Consolidation in Southern Europe*. London: Routledge.

Schecter, D. (1991) *Gramsci and the Theory of Industrial Democracy*. Aldershot: Avebury.

Schmidt, B. C. (2018) 'Hegemony: A conceptual and theoretical analysis', *Dialogue of Civilizations Research Institute, Expert Comment* (August): https://doc-research.org/2018/08/hegemony-conceptual-theoretical-analysis.

Schwarzmantel, J. (2015) *The Routledge Guidebook to Gramsci's Prison Notebooks*. Abingdon: Routledge.

Shore, C. (1990) *Italian Communism: The Escape from Leninism*. London: Pluto.

Sim, S. (2000) *Post-Marxism: An Intellectual History*. London: Routledge.

Smith, A. M. (1994) *New Right Discourse on Race and Sexuality: Britain, 1968–1990*. Cambridge University Press.

Stokes, D. (2018) 'Trump, American hegemony and the future of the liberal international order', *International Affairs* 94(1): 133–50.

Togliatti, P. (1976) *Lectures on Fascism*. New York: International Publishers.

Togliatti, P. (1979) *On Gramsci and Other Writings*. London: Lawrence & Wishart.

Tønder, L. and Thomassen, L. (eds.) (2005) *Radical Democracy: Politics Between Abundance and Lack*. Manchester University Press.

Torfing, J. (1998) *Politics, Regulation, and the Modern Welfare State*. Basingstoke: Macmillan.

Torfing, J. (1999) *New Theories of Discourse: Laclau, Mouffe and Žižek*. Oxford: Blackwell.

Tormey, S. (2015) *The End of Representative Politics*. Cambridge: Polity.

Townshend, J. (2003) 'Discourse theory and political analysis: A new paradigm from the Essex school?' *British Journal of Politics and International Relations* 5(1): 129–42.

Urbinati, N. (1998) 'From the periphery of modernity: Antonio Gramsci's theory of subordination and hegemony', *Political Theory* 26(3): 370–91.

Vacca, G. (2020) *Alternative Modernities: Antonio Gramsci's Twentieth Century*. Basingstoke: Palgrave Macmillan.

Wallerstein, I. (2004) *World-System Analysis: An Introduction*. London: Duke.

Waltz, K. N. (1979) *Theories of International Politics*. London: Addison-Wesley.

Watson, A. (2007) *History and Hegemony*. London: Routledge.

Webb, M. C. and Krasner, S. D. (1989) 'Hegemonic stability theory: An empirical assessment', *Review of International Studies* 15(2): 183–98.

Wenman, M. (2013) *Agonistic Democracy: Constituent Power in the Era of Globalisation*. Cambridge University Press.

Williams, R. (1961) *The Long Revolution*. London: Penguin.

Williams, R. (ed.) (1968) *May Day Manifesto 1968*. London: Penguin.

Williams, R. (1977) *Marxism and Literature*. Oxford University Press.

Williams, R. (2001) 'Culture is ordinary' [1958] in J. Higgins (ed.) *The Raymond Williams Reader*. Oxford: Blackwell.

Worth, O. (2015) *Rethinking Hegemony*. London: Macmillan Education – Palgrave.

Index

affect 66, 104–8
Agamben, Giorgio 108
agonism 73, 109, 110
Althusser, Louis 41–2, 48
anarchism 12, 99–100, 102,
    107, 109–10, 112
anarchy, international 77–8,
    79
Anderson, Perry 39–40, 42
antagonism
    contemporary 72–3
    Laclau and Mouffe's
        conception 65–6, 76, 98,
        101, 102, 111
    and left populism 74–5
Apartheid (South Africa) 11,
    68
Argentina 54

Bennett, Jane 109
biopolitics 105, 107
Black Lives Matter 70
Blair, Tony 56
Bolsheviks 10, 14, 17, 18, 32
Brazil 99
Brexit 92
Bull, Hedley 81

Catholic Church 15
Centre for Contemporary
    Cultural Studies (CCCS)
    48
Chávez, Hugo 54
China 55, 81
Chomsky, Noam 78
Christian Democrat Party
    (Italy) 33
civil society
    and contemporary counter-
        hegemony 94
    global 84, 86
    Gramsci's conception 20–4,
        86
    and party strategy 28, 33
    see also state
Clark, Ian 78, 81–2, 86, 87–8
Cold War 11, 32, 38, 58, 60,
    70, 74, 80, 87
Communist Manifesto 21
Communist Party of Italy (PCI)
    17–18, 32–4
Connolly, William 103, 106–7,
    109
consent
    absence of 16, 59, 91–2

consent (*cont.*)
  and class rule 4, 13, 19,
    20–4
  and force/coercion 9, 14–15,
    22–3, 30, 34–5, 78, 95,
    105, 114
  and globalization 90
  and intellectuals 25
  and international politics
    78–82, 84–6
  and 'the political' 73–4
  postwar consensus 36, 37–9,
    40, 48, 53, 55, 56, 59
  rebuilding social bases of 11,
    49–56
  and revolution 10, 13
  see also force
Conservative Party (UK) 50
counter-hegemony 92–4, 67,
    97, 112
Cox, Robert W. 11, 83–6, 93
crisis
  financial (2008–) 55, 74
  of interwar institutions 35
  in Marxism 60
  organic 34
  and populism 55
  of postwar state 38, 39, 43,
    44, 46–9, 50, 51, 53
  refugee 92
  social 9, 20–1, 54, 69
  Suez 40
  in US authority 87
cultural studies 8, 11, 46–9,
    54
culture
  and hegemony 4, 8–9, 23,
    35, 104
  and intellectual elites 25–6,
    39–40
  Italian 16, 19
  national 11, 50, 56, 85, 90,
    115
  neoliberal 111

popular 46–9
wars 92
see also discourse; ideology
Cutler, A. Claire 89

Day, Richard 99, 109
Deleuze, Gilles 102–3
democracy
  cosmopolitan 91, 94
  and ethics 9–10
  radical 2, 11, 58–76, 94,
    100, 108–9
  representative
    (parliamentary) 18, 32–4,
    37, 71–2, 110
  in revolutionary party 28–9,
    33–4
  social 38, 44, 51
  workers' 17
Derrida, Jacques 60, 61–2, 63,
    65
discourse
  and critics of hegemony
    104–7
  and Derrida 61–2
  and Foucault 60–1
  global 90
  International Relations 82
  liberal 72
  and Post-Marxism 2, 11, 58,
    64–6, 67–70, 76, 90, 102

ecologism 59, 72
elite
  and cultural studies 46–7
  culture 39–40
  and 'empirical' theories of
    the state 43
  and ethics of leadership 9,
    27
  and Gramsci's theory of
    intellectuals 25–7
  and international hegemony
    82, 84, 85, 89, 92, 93

Italian 15, 17, 24–5
and populism 54–5, 69,
74–5, 92
and postwar consensus 37
Empire
British 40, 80
global 103, 107, 111
empty signifier 69, 98
Engels, Friedrich 3
essentialism 58, 62–3, 64, 76,
101
ethics
of commitment 108–10
and counter-hegemony 93
and Derrida 62
and hegemony 5, 9–10, 76,
95
and radical democracy 71–4,
76
revolutionary 27–9, 31
European Social Forum 93
European Union 68, 81

Fascism 13, 17–18, 30, 31, 32,
34, 42, 43, 66
Femia, Joseph 29
feminism 59, 63, 72
First World War 17, 83
Floyd, George 70
force (coercive) 7, 9, 13,
14–15, 16, 20–4, 30, 37,
80, 86
see also consent; power;
violence
Ford, Henry 28
Fordism 28, 46, 88–9
Forgacs, David 70
Foucault, Michel 60–1, 62, 63,
64, 105, 106
Fox News 55
French Revolution 22, 40

gender 56
Germany 17

Gilbert, Jeremy 102, 112–13
Gill, Stephen 88–9
globalization 11, 58, 82–3,
87–95, 99, 112
governmentality 105
Gramsci, Antonio 3–4, 5, 8,
10, 13–35, 37, 38, 40,
48, 49, 64, 70, 75, 77,
82–6, 91, 93, 94, 98, 99,
113
Greece 75
Guattari, Félix 102, 103

Habermas, Jürgen 67
Hall, Stuart 8, 46–9, 51–4, 56,
64
Hardt, Michael 103, 107, 111
Hegel, Georg Wilhelm Friedrich
21
hegemonic stability theory 80,
86
*Hegemony and Socialist
Strategy* 63–73
historic bloc 15, 24, 85, 88,
93
Hobbes, Thomas 6, 7, 81
Hungary 17

ideology
and Althusser 42
and capitalism 11, 49, 58
and class 24, 31, 37, 41, 63,
90
and cultural studies 46–9
and discourse 65, 67–9
and globalization 88, 91, 92
and Hall 49, 51–4, 56
and international hegemony
81, 85, 86
as mechanism of consent 4,
104, 115
and Poulantzas 44
and revolutionary party 17,
31

ideology (*cont.*)
  and subjectivity 8–9, 19,
    24–7
  and state 38, 39, 41, 45,
    56–7
  and superstructure 24, 41
  and Thatcherism 50–4, 56
  and Williams 46
  see also culture; discourse;
    subjectivity
Indignados movement (Spain)
  99
intellectuals
  Gramsci's theory of 19,
    24–7
  Italian 16, 18
  New Left 46
  and populism 55
  and Post-Marxist theory of
    power 76
  and the revolutionary party
    28–9, 33

Jacobin
  club 22
  force 27
  imaginary 72, 108
Jessop, Bob 44–5, 51–4, 56

Kirchner, Cristina Fernández
  de 74
Kirchner, Néstor 74

Labour Party (UK) 52, 56, 74
labourism 39, 52, 59
Lacan, Jacques 60–3, 68, 101
Laclau, Ernesto 11, 54, 63–76,
  94, 101, 102, 108–9, 111,
  113
  see also Mouffe
language 8–9, 19, 23, 24, 25,
  51, 60, 61–2, 65, 103
Lash, Scott 103, 105, 106
Latin America 54–5, 63, 75

Law, David 88–9
Lenin, Vladimir Ilyich 14, 17,
  22, 27, 29, 71, 83, 100
Lyotard, Jean-François 60

Machiavelli, Niccolò 6–7, 14,
  19, 27, 79, 81
Macmillan, Harold 40
Marx, Karl 3
Marxism
  and class 21, 24, 30, 90
  and culture 46–9
  and economic determinism
    11, 16–17, 19, 23, 37, 57,
    114
  Gramsci's 14, 22–4, 31, 33
  and International Relations
    82–6
  and Laclau and Mouffe
    63–7, 68
  as a political ideology 28, 34,
    60, 62–3, 70, 100
  Russian 14
  and the state 10–11, 21,
    22–4, 36–57
  western 37, 59
  see also ideology; Jessop;
    Lenin; Post-Marxism;
    structuralism
Marxism Today 51
May Day Manifesto 38
Mazzini, Giuseppe 16
Miliband, Ralph 43
Modern Prince 19, 27–9, 94,
  108
Mosca, Gaetano 25
Mouffe, Chantal 11, 63–76, 94,
  101, 102, 108–9, 111, 113
  see also Laclau
Mussolini, Benito 13, 17, 18

Nairn, Tom 39–40, 42
national popular 4, 27, 30, 86,
  98, 113

Nazism 31, 43
Negri, Antonio 103, 107, 111
neo-liberalism 11, 54, 74–5,
    88–95, 103, 105, 106,
    110–12
New Left Review 39
new materialists 12, 102
New Right 59, 63
Newman, Saul 99–100, 106,
    107–8, 110

Occupy movement 93, 99
ontology 12, 97, 100–4, 111

Pareto, Vilfredo 25
passive revolution 15, 27, 91,
    93
Perón, Juan 54, 63
pluralism 10, 11, 58, 67, 70–4,
    76, 94, 99–100, 108–9
Podemos 75
populism 11, 49–56, 63,
    69–70, 74–5, 92, 94, 98
post-anarchism *see* anarchism
post-hegemony 97
Post-Marxism 2, 11, 57,
    58–76, 90, 94, 99, 100
post-structuralism 62, 64, 67,
    101
Poulantzas, Nicos 42–4, 48, 51
Powell, Enoch 48
power
    bloc 43, 53, 89
    destituent 107–8
    and domination 1–5, 11, 35,
        41, 102–3, 114
    and Foucault 60–1
    and Laclau and Mouffe 76
    and ontology 100–4
    seizure of 14, 15, 18, 30
    as a strategic concept 5–7,
        96–100, 111, 114
    world 11, 77–82, 94–5
Prison Notebooks 18, 19–32

race 38, 48, 52, 56, 63, 67, 68,
    70, 75, 92
Rawls, John 73
Reagan, Ronald 50, 59
realism, in International
    Relations theory 79–82,
    83, 85, 87
Republican Party (US) 56
Russian Federation 81
Russian Revolution 14, 17, 33,
    34

Sassoon, Donald 34
Second World War 35
sexuality 63, 67, 68, 72
socialism 16, 18, 33, 34, 39,
    50, 58–60, 71, 73
Stalin, Joseph V. 27, 29, 33, 38
Stalinism 31–2
state
    ancient 4, 77
    authoritarian 43, 52–3, 71
    British 39–40, 42–3, 48, 65
    building 10, 14, 19, 20–4,
        25, 27, 40, 76, 97–8
    capitalist 2, 10, 11, 18, 20,
        35, 36–57, 67, 70, 83–6,
        98
    and civil society 20–4, 76,
        114
    ethical 21, 24
    integral 15
    and international system 11,
        77–95
    Italian 15–18
    Latin American 54
    nation 4, 77–95, 98–9, 103,
        111, 115
    and power/domination 1, 3,
        7, 38–9, 97–103, 105–6,
        110, 112
    and revolution 123, 14, 30
    welfare 11, 35–7, 50–1, 85
    workers' 17

structuralism 41–5, 68
subjectivity 5–10, 19, 24, 30,
    42, 44, 47, 60–1, 64, 66,
    67–70, 76, 90–2, 95, 104–8
    see also culture; discourse;
    ideology
superstructure 20, 24, 56, 93
Syria 92

Taksim Gezi Park protests 99
Taylor, Frederick W. 28
Thatcher, Margaret 50, 51, 52,
    53, 56, 59, 74
Thatcherism 11, 45, 49–56, 64,
    65, 66, 98
Thompson, E. P. 46
Togliatti, Palmiro 31–4, 35
Trump, Donald 55–6, 69–70,
    92

UK (United Kingdom) 38, 46,
    48, 50, 59, 74, 92
United Nations 88

USA 28, 32, 33, 38, 50, 55–6,
    59, 69–70, 77, 78, 80, 81,
    82, 84, 86, 87–8, 92, 93
USSR (Soviet Union) 27, 32,
    33, 34, 41, 60, 80, 87, 93

Venezuela 54
violence 3, 4, 9, 17, 21, 22, 30,
    32, 35, 62, 81

Wallerstein, Immanuel 83
war of manoeuvre (or
    movement) 15, 23, 34, 93
war of position 15, 23, 33, 34,
    85, 113
Washington Consensus 89
Williams, Raymond 8, 46–8
World Social Forum 99
World Trade Organization
    (WTO) 89, 99
Worth, Owen 86

Zapatista communities 93